Exploring the Yukon River

Exploring the Yukon River

Archie Satterfield

AN AUTHORS GUILD BACKINPRINT.COM EDITION

Exploring the Yukon River

All Rights Reserved © 1979, 2000 by Archie Satterfield

No part of this book may be reproduced or transmitted in any form or by any means, graphic, electronic, or mechanical, including photocopying, recording, taping, or by any information storage or retrieval system, without the permission in writing from the publisher.

AN AUTHORS GUILD BACKINPRINT.COM EDITION

Published by iUniverse.com, Inc.

For information address:
iUniverse.com, Inc.
620 North 48th Street, Suite 201
Lincoln, NE 68504-3467
www.iuniverse.com

Originally published by Stackpole

ISBN: 0-595-14630-9

Printed in the United States of America

To Cassandra, Erin and Scott,
who went down the river with us,
and to Sarah,
who joined us for the lake trip.

Contents

Preface   ix
Introduction to the Yukon River   1
   The Journey   2
   The River   2
   History and Prehistory   2
   The Gold Rush   4
   Railroad and Steamboat   8
   The Atlin Strike   9
Trip Planning   11
   Access Points   11
   Where to Write for Information   12
   Customs Regulations   12
   Fire Permits and Licenses   12
   Kinds of Boats   13
   Safe Travel   15
   Equipment   16
   Clothing   17
   Bags   17
   Time Allowance   17
   Weather   18
   Boating Season   19
Headwaters—Bennett to Tagish   21
   Bennett   21
   Lake Bennett   25
   Carcross   25
   Nares Lake   26
   Tagish Lake   27
   Side Trip Down Windy Arm   28
   Tagish Lake North of Taku Arm   28
   Tagish   28

Headwaters—Atlin to Tagish   31
　Atlin   31
　Lake Atlin   32
　Atlin River   36
　Taku   37
　Grahame Inlet   38
　Golden Gate, Entrance to Taku Arm   38
　Taku Arm, South from Golden Gate   38
　Ben-My-Chree   39
　Taku Arm, North from Golden Gate   41
　Tagish Lake   42
　Tagish Lake North of Taku Arm   42
　Tagish   42
Marsh Lake to Whitehorse   45
　Source of the Yukon   46
　The River Begins   46
　Canyon City   47
　Miles Canyon   47
　Schwatka Lake   49
　Whitehorse   51
Whitehorse to Hootalinqua   55
　Takhini River   55
　Lake Laberge   55
　Lower Laberge   61
　Thirtymile River   61
　Hootalinqua   64
Hootalinqua to Carmacks   67
　Big Salmon   67
　Little Salmon   71
　Carmacks   74

Carmacks to Fort Selkirk 77
   Five Finger Rapids 77
   Tatchun Creek 81
   Rink Rapids 81
   Sam McGee's Ashes 81
   Yukon Crossing 82
   Minto 82
   Arrival at Fort Selkirk 84
   History—A Trading Post and
     Government Station 84
   The Remains of Old Fort Selkirk 89

Fort Selkirk to Stewart Island 93
   Camps, Way Stations and
     Creeks Below Selkirk 93
   White River 99
   Stewart Island 101

Stewart Island to Dawson City 107
   Sixtymile River 107
   Klondike River 109
   Dawson City 109

Tributary Rivers 119
   Teslin River 119
   Big Salmon River 120
   Pelly River 121
   Macmillan River 123
   White River 124
   Stewart River 125
   Sixtymile River 127

Suggested Reading 129

Index 131

Preface

When I was a child in the Missouri Ozarks, my father subscribed to a series of hunting, fishing and exploring magazines, and one of my childish daydreams was to move to Canada and live on a lake or river and paddle a canoe through the wilderness. Thirty years later I made my first trip in Canadian waters, not as the lone figure in a magazine illustration but as a city resident taking his young children on a wilderness trip. ("What?" Our friends almost shouted, "You took a *five-year-old* girl on a canoe trip in the Yukon?")

We stumbled and fumbled our way through the headwater lakes and down the river, largely ignorant of what to expect around the next bend, and weren't always certain if what we saw was of any historical significance. So I took hundreds of photographs on the two initial trips, then headed to the library and bookstores when we returned to learn, in too-typical tourist fashion, where we had been and what we had seen. A third trip two years later was more helpful, even though I was traveling in a large group and it was so cold and rainy that much of the trip was spent huddled beneath ponchos and tarps.

This book is a result of those trips and the need for a practical guide and layman history of the river from headwaters to the Klondike gold fields. The entire area is slowly developing into an international park between the United States and Canada commemorating the Klondike gold rush of 1897-98. The American portion was dedicated in 1976 and includes the overland routes of White Pass and Chilkoot Pass with much of downtown Skagway included, plus an interpretative center in Seattle. The Canadian government, under the auspices of Parks Canada, has been working toward a counterpart in Canada and extensive restoration work has been done in Dawson City.

This book contains numerous detailed maps made especially for it, but anyone seriously planning a trip on the Yukon River or the headwater lakes will also want the Canadian government's excellent topographic maps of the area. Following is a list of the National Topographic Maps, with sheet numbers, for the areas described in the book. It is strongly recommended that travelers along this route carry the maps. The maps in the book will get you there; the topographic maps will entertain you along the way by showing you the surrounding area and naming mountains and other physical features en route.

Topographic maps are available from either the Canada Map Office, 615 Booth Street, KIA 0E9, Ottawa, Ontario, or Staff Geologist, Government of the Yukon Territory, Whitehorse, Y.T.

Lake Atlin, Grahame Inlet, Taku Arm, Lake Bennett, Nares Lake, Tagish Lake, Marsh Lake and Yukon River to Whitehorse: Atlin 104 N, Skagway 104 M, Whitehorse 105 D.

Yukon River, Whitehorse to Dawson City: Whitehorse 105 D, Laberge 105 E, Glenlyon 105 L, Carmacks 115 I, Snag 115 J, Stewart River 115 O, Dawson 116 B, 116 C.

Teslin River: Teslin 105 C, Whitehorse 105 D, Laberge 105 E, Glenlyon 105 L, Carmacks 115 I.

Big Salmon River: Quiet Lake 105 F, Laberge 105 E.

Pelly River: Quiet Lake 105 F, Tay River 105 K, Glenlyon 105 L, Carmacks 115 I.

Macmillan River: Tay River 105 K, Lansing 105 N, Mayo 105 M, Glenlyon 105 L.

White River: Snag 115 J, 115K; Stewart River, 115 N, 115 O.

Sixtymile River: Dawson 116 B, 116 C; Stewart River 115 N, 115 O.

Stewart River: Nadaleen 106 C, Lansing 105 N, Mayo 105 M, McQuesten 115 P, Stewart River 115 O.

The author would like to acknowledge the help of the following persons:

In Whitehorse: Karl Crosby, John Guldner, Ken Sillak, Don Sawatsky, Joy Denton, Brian Speers, Paul Lucier, Alan Innes-Taylor, Dennis Senger, Cal Waddington, G. I. Cameron, the project geologist's staff and several people whose names I did not get but who, nevertheless, helped with my travels there.

On the river: The Mountie in Carmacks for not attempting to arrest me when my young son asked, loudly, why I had not bought a fishing license (I wasn't fishing, but didn't want to tackle the chore of convincing a Mountie); Danny Roberts and his family at Fort Selkirk, for good company and information:

Rudy and Yvonne Burian at Stewart Island for information and a place to buy a candy bar where one would not expect a candy bar; Pete and Mary for tea and an insight into the new settlers along the river.

In Dawson City: Dick Stevenson, Roger Mendelsohn, John Gould, the late Mike Comadina, A. Fuhre and Mike Stutter.

In Vancouver, B.C.: Myron Laka and Marjorie Robertson, formerly of the Yukon House; Brian Martin, one of the best raconteurs to leave the Yukon; and Dennis Bell, formerly of the Canadian Press.

In Washington: *The Seattle Post-Intelligencer* and *The Seattle Times,* for permitting me to go to the Yukon on assignment when they knew I actually was playing; the National Park Service, Pacific Northwest Region; Ralph Munro, assistant to Governor Dan Evans, who virtually forced me to make one trip down the river.

In Atlin: Joe and Carol Florence for information and fantastic moose steaks; Stefan Shearer for guide services and companionship; the late Reg Brooks of Grahame Inlet for instructions and conversation late into the night.

In Skagway: Skip Burns for introducing me to the Chilkoot and the river.

Most of the historical photos in this book are from the Asahel Curtis Collection at the Washington State Historical Society Museum in Tacoma, Washington. Asahel Curtis was the younger brother of Edward S. Curtis, the famous photographer of North American Indians. Asahel went to the Klondike with the big rush in 1897-98 and photographed the entire stampede, from Seattle to Skagway, over Chilkoot and White passes, and down the Yukon River to the Klondike gold fields.

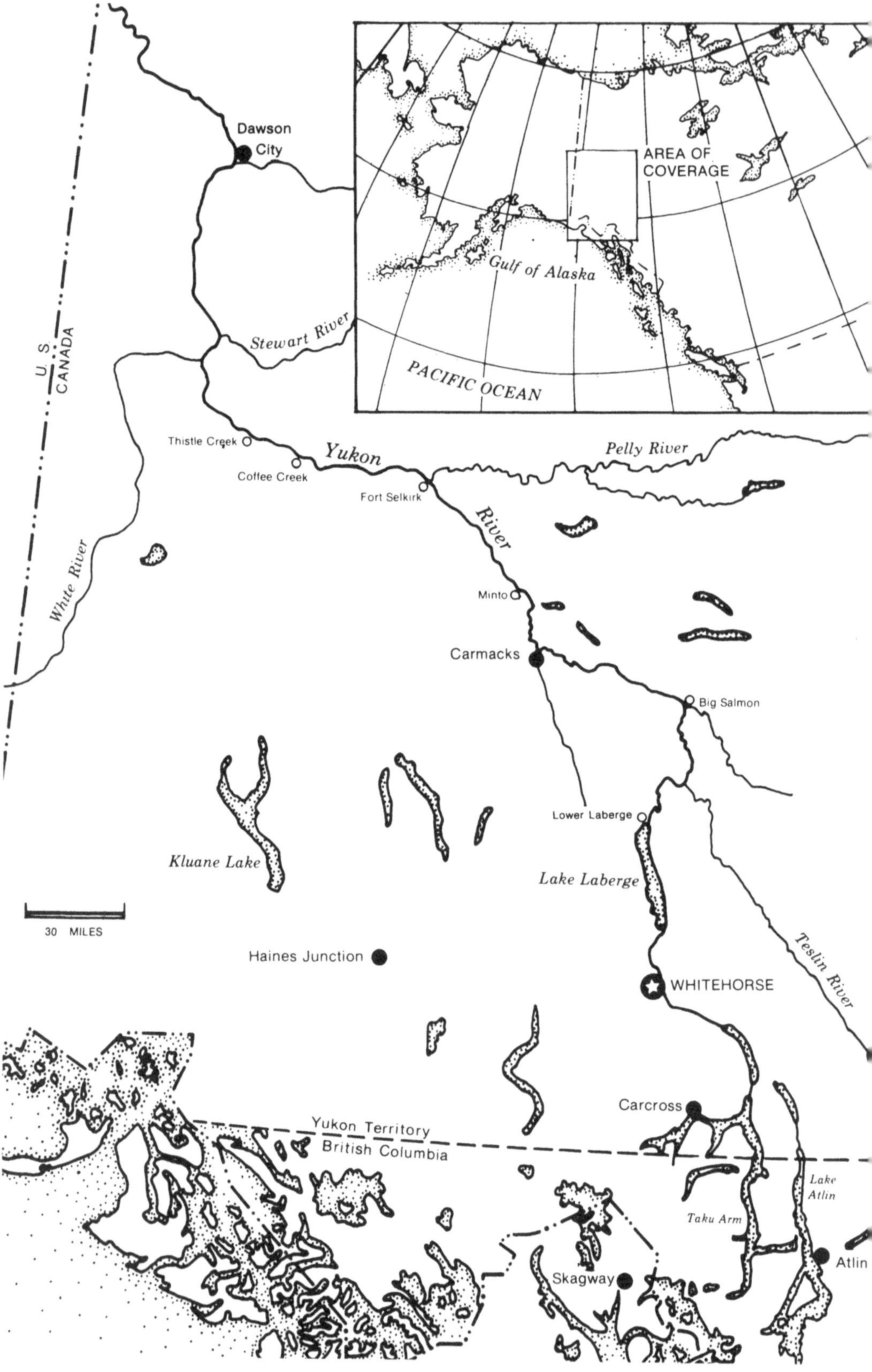

Dawson City
AREA OF COVERAGE
Gulf of Alaska
PACIFIC OCEAN
Stewart River
U.S.
CANADA
Thistle Creek
Coffee Creek
Yukon River
Fort Selkirk
Pelly River
White River
Minto
Carmacks
Big Salmon
Lower Laberge
Kluane Lake
Lake Laberge
30 MILES
Haines Junction
WHITEHORSE
Teslin River
Carcross
Yukon Territory
British Columbia
Lake Atlin
Taku Arm
Skagway
Atlin

Introduction to the Yukon River

During the past few years the Yukon River, after a respite of nearly 20 years, has again become a major transportation corridor through the Yukon Territory. From the Klondike gold rush of 1897-98 until the mid-1950s, when the spurs of the Alaska Highway were strung through the territory, the river was the only means of getting from the terminus of the White Pass & Yukon Route railhead at Whitehorse to the Klondike gold diggings outside Dawson City. After the highways put the paddlewheel riverboats out of business, the river route lay dormant until the early 1970s, when recreational boaters began following the historic route to Dawson City in increasing numbers.

At that time, no guide book existed. The only source of information was the set of maps used by steamboat skippers (which have been adapted and redrawn for this book) and a wild rivers survey, copies of which were given away by the Yukon government. The casual boater making the trip from headwaters to Dawson City had no information on the history or natural history of the area, no directory of what could be seen along the riverbank.

River traffic has doubled and trebled and is still increasing each summer. The numbers will continue to grow because of the establishment of the Klondike Gold Rush National Historical Park. Although the Klondike gold rush was the most dramatic event in Yukon history, its importance to the river has been offset in later years by the steamboat era that ran from the gold rush until the 1950s. Nearly all signs of human endeavor along the river are related to the steamboat years, and not to the gold rush itself.

The Journey
Some river enthusiasts might prefer going beyond Dawson City into Alaska—to Circle City or Eagle, or on down to the Tanana near Fairbanks. This book will not help them beyond Dawson City. I have chosen to limit it to that 600-mile stretch of lakes and river because of the Klondike park; because it makes a good two-week trip, long enough for the average boater on vacation; and because it is easier to leave the river at Dawson City for land transportation or air service.

The book concludes with brief descriptions of the various tributary rivers between Whitehorse and Dawson City.

The River
Ironies are like gold: They are where they are found. For now, we will limit ourselves to only two ironies concerning the Yukon River. Others will occur from time to time, like roils and sweepers and upwellings along the river.

First, the Yukon River begins almost within sight of the Pacific Ocean, yet it flows more than 2000 miles (3200 km) before it reaches that ocean. From Chilkoot or White Pass above Skagway, a look backward about 15 miles (24 km) will reveal the waters of Lynn Canal, a straight, narrow ribbon of Pacific Ocean saltwater that ends at Dyea Inlet, the foot of the Chilkoot Trail which leads into the Yukon system.

Second, the Yukon River undoubtedly was the first major North American river used by man, but the last discovered by the white man. This is not surprising, considering its course through a rather hostile environment that discouraged merchants and their traveling salesmen of two centuries ago. It is that same environment that today limits its use for recreational purposes to only about three months of the year.

History and Prehistory
Except for a few legends preserved by the Indians, little is known of life along the river before the advent of the record-keeping white men. Our accurate knowledge goes only to the first contact between the disparate cultures, and any records coming from that contact must be tempered with tolerance for cultural differences. In spite of our advanced knowledge and

reservoirs of information today, we still cannot always exercise tolerance. In the 17th and 18th centuries, it must have been virtually impossible.

Traditionally, the Indians of the North kept to the forests and left the treeless tundra and Arctic Coast to the Eskimos. In the Yukon and Northern British Columbia, there were five major Indian tribes: The Tagish in what is now the Whitehorse, Carcross and Tagish area; the Inland Tlingit; the coastal Tlingit in Southeast Alaska; the Tutchone, especially the northern branch, along the middle section of the Yukon River; and the Han in the Dawson City area.

Also playing a major role in the Yukon were the Chilkats of Lynn Canal, a branch of the Tlingits. The Chilkats were the middlemen in trading; they dealt with the Indians of the Interior, exchanging fish oil and white men's trade goods for furs, horns and other products.

Little is known about them, except that they had an extremely difficult life. Their life could be an example for those people from the southern part of the continent who plan to go north and live off the land. Stories from the Indians' oral history tell of widespread famines, deaths by freezing and occasional cannibalism to survive. Living off the land was, and still is, a risky way to live in the Yukon. The cash economy has much to recommend it if longevity, low infant mortality and general good health are one's goals in life. On a leisurely trip down the Yukon River in midsummer when the temperature may be up to 32°C (90°F), the sky filled with fluffy clouds, flowers growing in the rich valleys, and moose and bear seen on the river bank, then it is easy to think of the Yukon as a land of plenty.

The old-timers there will agree it is the land of plenty: Plenty cold, plenty months of temperatures below zero; and plenty work to do during the short summer preparing for winter, but seldom plenty of food.

No one could have agreed more than the first white men on the Yukon. The first was Robert Campbell, who established Fort Selkirk at the confluence of the Pelly River and the Yukon in 1843. Later, the Russians explored the upper river. The summers and autumns were pleasant enough, but the long, cold winters which confined the men to the tiny, smelly cabins for months on end were another matter. Considering the circumstances, one marvels that the white men, who had the choice, did not leave the employment of fur companies and head south to become farmers or clerks.

But it was fur, then gold, that brought the white men into the Yukon, and gold that finally caused the Yukon to be settled by permanent white residents, who altered the landscape and the social customs.

Scenes such as this were common on Seattle's waterfront during the gold rush of 1897-98, as "stampeders" struck off for the Klondike. This ship was the coastal steamer Roanoke.

The Gold Rush

The history of the gold rush will be told only briefly here because it has been told often elsewhere. The bibliography lists the major books on the subject.

There are a number of versions of how the first gold on the Yukon was discovered and by whom. Was it an employee of the Russian American Trading Co., of the Hudson's Bay Co., both of which were more interested in fur than gold? Or was it a minister, as some versions insist? No matter; the gold was discovered on different feeder streams, the word leaked out and a trickle of prospectors began heading north. One must bear in mind that 19th-century North America was addicted to gold rushes: There were gold rushes in Colorado and California and smaller ones in the Pacific Northwest. They were part of the social order.

It took several years for the biggest discovery, in the Klondike, to be made. In the meantime, prospectors worked the Yukon tributaries. They found gold at Circle City, Forty Mile, Stewart River and dozens of smaller places. There wasn't enough for a big stampede; only enough to keep the prospectors interested and to justify having trading posts operated by men with a gambling spirit themselves. These traders would continue grubstaking serious prospectors, taking their losses with their gains, always believing the next summer, the next stream, the next prospector would hit it.

They hit the big one in 1896, when a white man named George Washington Carmack and two Indians, Tagish Charlie and Skookum Jim, the latter his brother-in-law, made the great Klondike discovery on August 16 on a stream called Rabbit Creek—immediately renamed Bonanza Creek.

The town of Forty Mile was abandoned as the miners rushed upstream against the swift current, poling and tracking their boats to the Klondike River and up it a short distance to the Bonanza and other streams feeding the small river. One of the traders, Joseph LaDue, set up a sawmill where the Klondike empties into the Yukon and established a town named for George M. Dawson, a Canadian geologist and explorer who was sent to the Yukon in 1887.

The Klondike strike was the dream come true for prospectors. During the remainder of that summer and through the winter they took gold out by the pound. When summer returned and the ice cleared from the river, many were ready to return to their homes and families (most were from the United States).

After they "cleaned up"—separated the gold from the dirt they dug that winter—they caught paddlewheelers down the Yukon to the Bering Sea at St. Michael, Alaska, and crowded aboard ships for home. Thus, it was 11 months after the strike before the rest of the world knew of the event.

This gold dredge was abandoned on its way down the Yukon.

The first ship to arrive was the *Excelsior,* which landed in San Francisco loaded with a group of miners on July 15, 1897. But it wasn't until the coastal steamer *Portland* landed in Seattle two days later that the full impact of the strike was understood. A newspaper reporter coined the magic words: "A ton of gold." That started the last, great gold rush and took several thousand inexperienced persons to a place none had heard of, in a climate with a temperature range of 38°C (100°F) or more.

There were various routes from the United States and southern Canada to the Klondike; many were promoted by greedy townspeople and steamship lines without regard for the hardships worked on the travelers. Some stampeders went up through the interior of Canada from Edmonton, Alberta, an impossible route that killed most of those attempting it. The inland route from Ashford, British Columbia, was equally hazardous. Two others were the Malaspina Glacier route from Alaska and the Copper River route from Cook Inlet. The "rich man's route" was from Seattle to St. Michael and up the Yukon River; it took more than a year. The routes over the Chilkoot and White Passes are well known.

These latter two were the shortest, probably the easiest when all alternatives are considered, but certainly no wilderness jaunt. The routes seemed simple. The stampeders took ships from San Francisco, Seattle, Vancouver and Victoria up the Inside Passage to the head of Lynn Canal, landing at Skagway and Dyea. From Skagway, they went over White Pass only 40 miles (64 km) to Lake Bennett. From Dyea, 9 miles (14 km) from Skagway, they went 26 miles (42 km) to Lake Lindeman, or 8 miles (13 km) farther to Lake Bennett.

Once over the passes, they had no more walking to do. The rest of the trip was by boat, down the chain of lakes and into the Yukon River, then north to Dawson City and the Klondike gold fields. Simple?

Not really. First, they had to get roughly a ton of gear from tidewater at Skagway and Dyea over the passes to the lakes. The Canadian Mounties posted at the summits of the passes, on the international boundary, required each person to bring in at least a year's supply of food; other supplies they required brought the weight to 1150 pounds (522 kg). Add to that the clothing, tools, firearms, etc., that each person would bring, and it roughed out at a ton: a ton of gear for the fabled "ton of gold" that was brought to Seattle.

This had to be either carried on the owner's back or a back he hired to carry it. There were packers with strings of horses and mules on White Pass, but the cost was as high as the market would bear. Horses could not operate well in the Chilkoot because it was too rough. Enterprising businessmen built aerial tramways. In the early stages of the gold rush, Chilkat Indians hired out as packers, but they gradually priced themselves out of business.

This was only part of it. Other harsh facts included the wintering over in the mountains with the blizzards that are common, frigid winds, low temperatures, epidemics of spinal meningitis, theft, murder and avalanches.

After the stampeders got themselves and their gear to the lakes, they then had to build or buy boats. They had to saw the scrawny green spruce and pine and build a craft that would get them through the lakes, down the river, through the rapids at Miles Canyon and below, then on down the river. Today stumps two and three meters high are found around Lakes Lindeman and Bennett, showing where the trees were felled when deep snow covered the ground.

During that mad winter of 1897-98, stampeders were strung out along the trail all the way from tidewater over the passes, alongside Lake Bennett, Tagish Lake, Marsh Lake and down the river to Lake Laberge and beyond. All were waiting for the ice to clear from the river and lakes. Those below Lake Laberge were the first to get under way in the spring of 1898, since the river ice clears first.

By the second week of June, the scraggly armada began arriving in Dawson City, all 7000-odd boats and rafts. But they were presented with a bad joke. In spite of their efforts during the past several months, all the claims worth staking had been taken by prospectors already in the Yukon. For most, the gold rush was an exercise in futility. Many caught the first paddlewheeler back down the Yukon to St. Michael, Alaska, and home. Others stayed to work for wages because they had no more money. The great gold rush became a bittersweet memory.

Railroad and Steamboat

In the meantime, another enterprise was underway that would give permanence to the Yukon River as a transportation corridor. A railroad, part of the White Pass & Yukon Route, was being built under extremely hazardous circumstances over White Pass. The narrow-gauge rails were stretched to Lake Bennett, which took the walking out of the passes for prospectors and animals (which by the way, had died by the thousands), and past the treacherous Miles Canyon, Whitehorse and Squaw Rapids to a spot where steamboats from downriver could land.

Thus began the steamboat and railroad era of the Yukon that lasted until the early 1950s, when highways were built and air service established. The railroad still exists and probably always will. The steamboats have disappeared from the river.

But for more than 50 years, the steamboats were there. More than 200 were built and operated on the river at different times. They hauled passengers, ore, supplies, and you-name-it between Dawson City and Whitehorse. From Whitehorse to the ocean at Skagway, the narrow-gauge trains took over.

The Atlin Strike

While the WP&YR railroad was under construction, a gold strike was made on the other side of the Coast Range near Lake Atlin.

There is a romantic story which tells us Fritz Miller and Kenneth McLaren took a wrong turn somewhere on Chilkoot or White Pass and ended up in the Atlin district. Shrugging, they started panning just the same, and lo! gold.

Unfortunately, that is not the case. Nor is it true that a dying prospector with a sack of gold and a rough map led to the discovery there.

The facts seem to be that Fritz Miller's brother, George, went over the Juneau Icecap to Lake Atlin in 1896 and found "colors." Two years later, in January, 1898, Fritz Miller and Ken McLaren went over to check the prospects for themselves. They found gold on Pine Creek, and the rush to Atlin began soon after. When word leaked out, the crews working on the White Pass & Yukon Route roadbed began a mass exodus to Atlin, walking off the job with nearly all the railroad's shovels and picks in hand.

Later, the Atlin mining followed the course of the Klondike gold fields, and hand labor by individual miners was replaced by corporate endeavor and huge dredges.

The steamboat era that followed the gold rush at Dawson City and Atlin and lasted 50-odd years figured prominently on the headwater lakes. The railroad took care of the major problem of Miles Canyon and the rapids just below it, so that there were two separate steamboat routes: One for the Yukon River from Whitehorse downstream, and a second for the lake system from Carcross back to the foot of the Coast Range.

After the railroad was completed, the paddlewheel steamboats on Lake Bennett could not survive. Small boats served the mines and towns on the headwater lakes until the Alaska Highway and its system of spur roads were built. The small lake boats ran down the chain of lakes between Carcross and Taku, where a railroad—actually little more than a tramway—was built.

This railroad was the shortest line in Canada at the time, and — at just over two miles (three km)—certainly one of the shortest in the world. It was built to transport cargo from the Grahame Inlet station called Taku up the riverbank to Lake

Atlin's Scotia Bay, where other steamboats were waiting to load the cargo. The tiny train engine, named "The Duchess," ran forward one way, and reverse the other.

"The Duchess" and the last remaining lake boat, the *Tutshi*, can be seen on the lake shore at Carcross. In Atlin, the lake steamboat *Tarahne* has been beached on Atlin's waterfront and is being restored by the local historical society.

Relics from paddlewheeler days are on display at Carcross.

Trip Planning

Access Points

There are several alternatives for those who do not wish to make the entire Klondike trip in one outing, or those who do not have the time. Following is a list of access points for the headwater lakes and the Yukon River itself. Tributary rivers are described in the last chapter of the book.

The headwater lakes can be reached from the following points: *Bennett Station*—Access only by White Pass & Yukon Route daily train. *Carcross*—Access by railroad and a spur off the Alaska Highway that runs from Whitehorse to Carcross and connects with the highway again at Tagish. *Tagish*—On the Alaska Highway. *Atlin*—At the end of a 61-mile (98-km) spur off the Alaska Highway, and 110 miles (177 km) from Whitehorse.

The main stem of the Yukon River can be reached from all the access points listed for the lakes; the closest is Tagish. Other access points, beginning at Marsh Lake, are as follows: *Alaska Highway Bridge*—Just below Marsh Lake and above the Marsh Lake dam. *Miles Canyon*—A campground just below the canyon and a dock near the hydroelectric dam. *Rotary Park, Whitehorse*—Just below the dam and near the steamboat *Klondike*. *Takhini River*—North of Whitehorse about five miles (eight km). *Lake Laberge Campground*—On the Klondike Highway opposite Richtofen Island. *Carmacks*—109 miles (175 km) north of Whitehorse by Klondike Highway; 202 miles (325 km) by river; 250 miles (415 km) to Dawson City by river. *Minto*—56 miles (90 km) by river from Carmacks; approximately 40 miles (64 km) by highway, 202 miles (325 km) by river, to Dawson City.

Where to Write for Information

Your best source of information for the lake and river system is the Yukon government: Director, Travel and Information, Box 2703, Whitehorse, Yukon Territory, Canada. This department will provide you with information on transportation, canoe and boat rentals, charter buses, lodging, etc.

Other sources include: Board of Trade, Atlin, British Columbia; White Pass & Yukon Route, Whitehorse, Y.T.; Whitehorse Chamber of Commerce; Klondike Visitors Association, Dawson City, Y.T.; Yukon Canoe Rental, 507 Alexander Street, Whitehorse, Y.T.

Customs Regulations

The major customs regulations for Americans to remember when entering Canada are that no handguns are permitted in that country; and you can bring only two days' food per person into the country. You can bring rifles and shotguns into the country with no problem, however, and so far as food is concerned, you'll have no difficulty finding a wide variety in Whitehorse. The selection obviously is narrower in the smaller towns, but you will find all the staples in Atlin, Carcross, Tagish and Carmacks. However, food will be more expensive in the smaller towns than in Whitehorse because of the cost of transportation.

Fire Permits and Licenses

Fire permits must be obtained from Royal Canadian Mounted Police offices for trips into the wilderness. There are no particular problems involved in obtaining them, and it is a good opportunity to ask further questions about your route and to register with the Mounties, also required by law. You simply fill out the form and include your destination, route and estimated time of arrival; remember to tell the Mounties when you arrive so no searches will be launched.

Fishing licenses are available at most stores along the way. On Lake Atlin, you will need both British Columbia and Yukon licenses since you will be traveling across the border.

Have proof of ownership for your boat and other expensive equipment, such as cameras. Americans may be asked to register cameras, firearms, boats and other similar gear on entering the country.

All artifacts in Canada are protected by federal law, including old bottles you might dig up, telegraph insulators found along the river, and even broken dishes and rusty buckets found at old woodcutters' camps. If you buy anything remotely like an artifact, be sure you have a receipt for it.

Kinds of Boats

Every kind of boat imaginable has navigated the Yukon River, including an amphibious automobile. Some locals consider it foolhardy to travel on the headwater lakes—and Lake Laberge—in anything other than a powered boat. They point out how rapidly severe storms can arrive on the lakes and catch you away from the shore, or away from a good place to land and hole up out of the storm. They also point out how far you will have to paddle when traveling from either Atlin or Bennett to the river.

When planning a trip on the lakes, it is essential that you allow extra time for storms and high winds, just as it is important that you seldom stray far from shore. There are fewer problems for paddlers on the river than on the lakes, yet the lakes are so beautiful that they should not be missed, either. Perhaps the best solution, if your time is limited, is to plan two trips, one for the river and another for the lakes.

With these limitations and prejudices in mind, following is a general rating of craft based on the author's personal experience and that of others he has talked to:

Kayaks

Many people use kayaks on both the lakes and the river, but they have obvious disadvantages. They are dangerous in heavy weather on the lakes, they are difficult to get into and out of, they do not carry much equipment, and what they do carry is usually beyond easy reach when needed. They are more practical on the river than lakes, and remember—on the lake portion of the trip you will be going across Lake Laberge, noted for its sudden and vicious squalls. There is virtually no whitewater on the trip to require the maneuverability advantages of a kayak.

Canoes These, too, are dangerous on the big lakes and are easy to swamp or flip in the heavy swells. However, on the river, they are great: silent, easy to paddle and cheaper to rent or transport. But bear in mind that the river and lake drownings during the past few years have been from canoes.

Inflatable Boats These are about evenly divided between pluses and minuses. They are virtually impossible to sink (in the case of the expensive models such as Zodiac and Avon) because they have so many flotation chambers. They are easy to transport to the North and very comfortable for sitting because any surface is a potential seat. They are equally good on the lakes and the river.

The minuses include their tendency to develop leaks ranging from pinpricks to gaping holes, and over to the bank you go for repairs. They have a tendency (with a 20-hp motor) to plow through the water, especially when attempting to run upstream, and their fuel consumption will be greater than that of a freight canoe or river boat because of the drag.

Freight Canoes These remarkable boats are the most stable, biggest and easiest of all to handle. The modified V-bottoms are the best for both lake and river, and they are incredibly tough and seaworthy; with a 22-footer you could almost go into the shipping business. Six or seven people and gear can easily fit into a 20- or 22-footer powered by a 20-hp motor, and they draw so little water that going aground in the river is no great problem. The author ranks these tops for both lake and river.

River Skiffs These flat-bottomed boats are a close second and would be first were it not for the inherent problems with a flat bottom. On the lakes they have a tendency to plow through, or under, the waves to drench you and they bounce and bob and plop across the heavy swells. They are best on the river. They offer more room than the freighters, haul more people per foot than a freighter and are the least likely of all powered boats to run aground. These are strongly recommended for a large party of congenial people. As with the freighters and canoes, they can be rented in Whitehorse, and for a group of six or eight preferring a powered boat, the cost would be minimal spread over the whole party.

As stated before, all types of boats have navigated the river and lakes in safety, but those traveling on the lakes in kayaks or canoes must be prepared for some tense moments. If the wind doesn't blow, they can return and accuse the author of cowardice. But for those who get swamped or worse, I'll say it now and never again: You were warned!

Safe Travel

There are numerous rules for safe travel by canoe or kayak, and these are the basic ones:

Don't travel alone. At least two vessels should be in a party, and preferably more. Be experienced in handling whatever vessel you use. Always wear a life jacket.

Be certain that all equipment is firmly lashed in to prevent its loss in a spill.

Watch for sudden changes in the weather, and if it looks bad, head for shore and make camp. Watch each other for signs of fatigue or the approach of hypothermia.

When camping overnight, place a stick at the water's edge so you will see changes in water level. Higher water levels often mean more trees, brush and other debris will be swept into the water.

Scout rapids, no matter how small they look. Go through rough water one vessel at a time with plenty of space between for rescue; stop below rough water and wait for the others to come through. Learn to read the river to avoid hitting submerged bars or trees.

If you capsize, stay with your boat and wait for help.

In case of a spill, it is imperative that you get dry as quickly as possible. Get ashore and build a fire immediately; strip off your wet clothes and put on dry ones. If possible, dry your wet clothes over the fire before proceeding on the river, so you will have spare dry clothes again.

It is wise to carry extra stove fuel for starting fires in such situations, rather than wasting precious time building a Boy Scout-type fire. The Indians on the river call gasoline "Indian fire starter," because they know the importance of starting a fire immediately when they get wet.

In case of trouble, stay near the river and keep a fire going. Your chances of getting help are much better on the river than they would be beating through the brush toward a highway, which could lead to your getting lost.

Equipment

A canoe or kayak should have a spray cover, which can double as a tarp in rainy weather. Have extra lines, 30 meters long, for bow and stern. Carry an extra paddle and a repair kit for the hull. Have a life jacket and knee pads for each person.

Map and compass.

Matches in a waterproof container. Fire starter, whether candles or chemical type. Knife. Ax or saw. Cooking and eating utensils. A stove and fuel; spares of both are advisable.

Food. Water. Carry water-purification tablets and a collapsible water jug that won't break or take up unnecessary room when it's not in use.

Tent with insect netting and a rain fly. Sleeping bag and insulating pad.

Sunglasses and an elastic band to keep them in place. Suntan lotion. Insect repellant. Mosquito coils. First aid kits.

Pack an emergency kit in a waterproof container and take it just in case the unthinkable happens. The 10 Essentials list developed by The Mountaineers years ago, and since expanded to 13 by Tim Kneeland, of Seattle, makes a good basic emergency kit. The kit should contain: Map, compass, flashlight, knife, matches, fire starter, extra clothing, extra food, water, first-aid kit, sunglasses and sunburn preventative, and emergency shelter (tube tent), and signalling devices. "Food" includes some wire for snares, a simple fishing kit, bouillon and chocolate, and some aluminum foil to cook in. Have paper and pencil.

Clothing

Be sure to have two changes of clothing (at least two), rain gear, long johns, and a hat or cap.

Everything possible should be woolen since it provides more warmth than any synthetic material, even when wet. Socks, underwear, pants and shirts should all be woolen. Extra lightweight shirts can be used when the weather is warm and dry, but woolen shirts or jackets should be kept handy.

Layer dressing is recommended to adjust to changes in temperature. For example, a wool jacket can be slipped over a lightweight shirt, and a parka or raingear over that. It can be removed in the same order as the weather warms.

Most important, always have a change of dry clothing with you, even if it means laying over at a campsite a few hours to get it dry.

For footwear, shoes that are impervious to dunking in the water should be worn while on the lakes or river, with an extra pair of hiking shoes in the pack for leg-stretching side hikes and warmth around the camp.

Bags

Have waterproof bags for *everything*—dry food and clothing are especially important. Some get by with soft backpacks (summit-types are fine) wrapped in waterproof bags.

Time Allowance

Following is only a rough estimation of the time involved in the various legs of the journey. The trips can be made faster or slower, depending on one's desires and time. However, these times allow for bad weather, frequent stops to poke around the shores and generally enjoying oneself.

Bennett to Whitehorse—3 days motoring, 5 days paddling.

Atlin to Whitehorse—No side trips: 4 days motoring, 6-8 days paddling. All side trips: 10 days motoring, 16-20 days paddling.

Whitehorse to Dawson—10-14 days motoring, 14-16 days paddling.

The sinister appearance of this poncho-clad group of travelers will vanish with the brief shower that caught them. Such rains are seldom bad enough to curtail activities.

Weather

The usual image of a Yukoner is a cross between Yosemite Sam and Santa Claus with icy beard and stoplight nose. Above him is a comic-strip ballon saying "Forty below and blowing," or something like that.

Don't you believe it. It certainly gets that cold in the winter, but you will be traveling in the summer when the days are long (24 hours of light in June), and you most likely will have temperatures up to 27°C (80°F) or even higher.

There is little rainfall in the Yukon interior through which the river flows and the annual average is about 30 centimeters/ 12 inches. However, you can expect showers and should be prepared.

There are exceptions, of course. For example, the summer we made the lake trip was wetter and colder than usual. Some nights in August were below freezing, and rainy, overcast weather was common. Again, you must be prepared with warm clothing, rain gear and waterproof tent fly.

Weather in the headwater lakes is totally unpredictable, can change in minutes and usually bears no relationship to regional forecasts from Juneau or Whitehorse, where radio stations issue forecasts. Old-timers predict the weather here by looking out the door. And if it is storming or looks as if it will, they stay off the lakes.

Boating Season

As a general rule, the boating season runs from mid-June until the end of September. The only *if* in June is if the ice has cleared from the lakes. Most years the ice is gone by June 10, but there are exceptions when the ice stays in the lakes until the third week of June. In this case, you will have to bypass the lakes and begin the trip at Whitehorse, since Lake Laberge usually clears ahead of the upper lakes because of the river at each end.

The river is usually high in June and slowly diminishes as the summer progresses. During the high-water period, the major problem is avoiding all the debris in the water—stumps, whole trees, garbage picked up on the river banks, etc. The river is faster at high-water periods with a flow up to 9 to 10 knots in places. By mid-summer, this drops to 5 to 7 knots in the portion of the river we are concerned with here.

By early September, the river is quite low and the risk of running aground increases. Also, the weather is more unpredictable and certainly colder. It is best to plan trips from mid-June through late August.

The shell of the church at Lake Bennett, a landmark since gold-rush days, has been restored by the Canadian government.

Headwaters
—Bennett to Tagish

Bennett

Bennett was the end of Chilkoot and White Pass trails during the gold rush, and today is a lunch-stop for passengers on the WP&YR. Trains from both Skagway and Whitehorse meet at Bennett during the noon hour, have lunch (part of your ticket price and all you can eat), and then continue on. The train crews are changed here; Canadian crews run between Bennett and Whitehorse, American crews between Bennett and Skagway.

When you arrive on the train, you first should retrieve all your gear from the baggage car before having lunch to be sure you aren't left standing alone on the roadbed watching your gear depart without you.

Only a few traces of the gold rush and railroad-building days remain around Bennett. The most prominent relic is the church on the hill looking down the lake. It was begun in 1899, when several hundred men were still at Bennett, some working on the railroad, others getting ready to head down the river to the Klondike or working in the shipyards building paddlewheelers, skiffs and rafts.

When the railroad was completed, the boatyards disappeared virtually overnight, and the church was left unfinished. The exterior was completed, but there are no interior walls or floors and the ceiling is not completed. The railroad and government have kept the church from gracefully falling in on itself, and funds have been allocated by the Canadian federal government to preserve it.

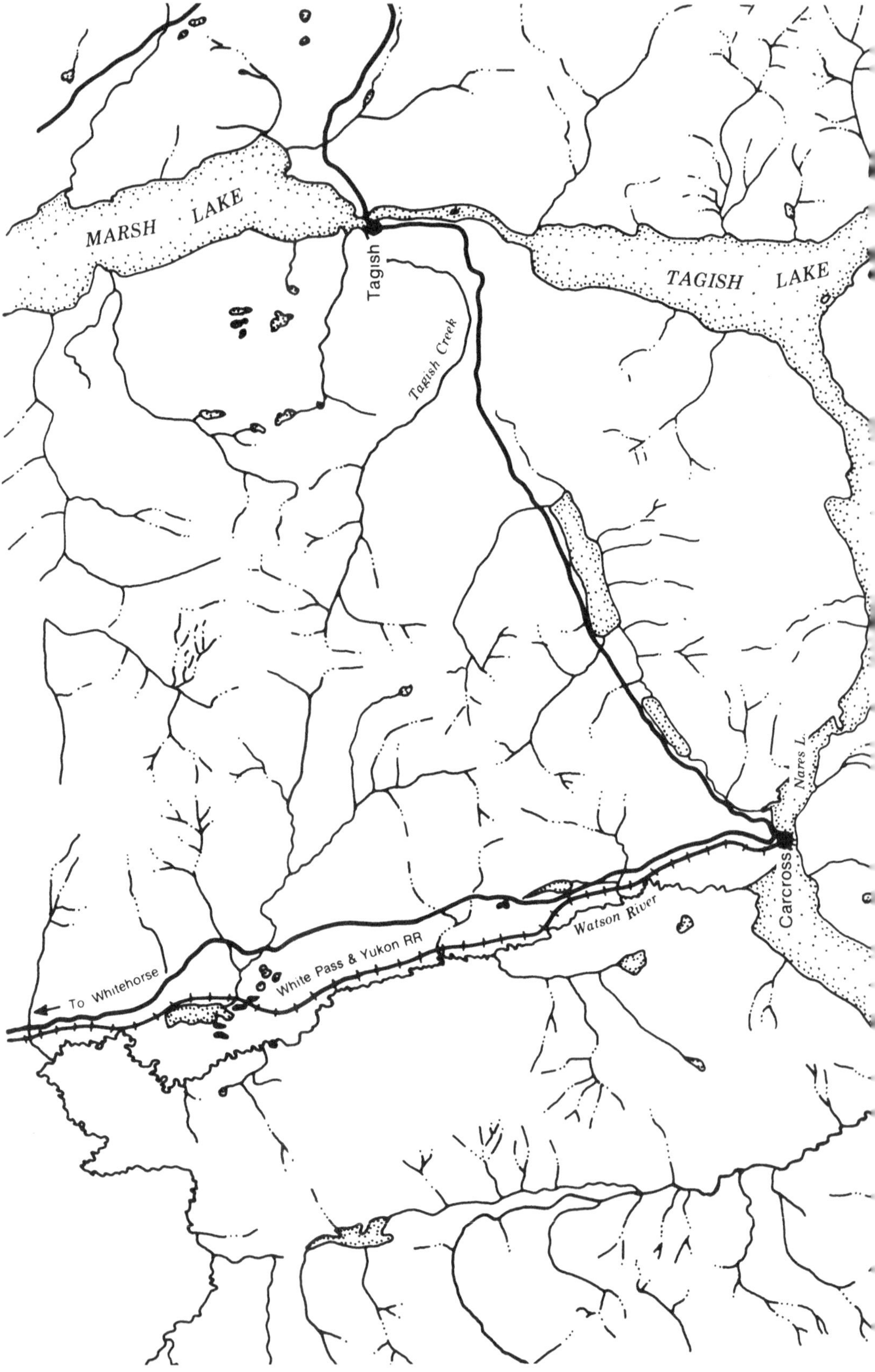
MARSH LAKE
Tagish
Tagish Creek
TAGISH LAKE
Nares L.
Carcross
Watson River
White Pass & Yukon RR
To Whitehorse

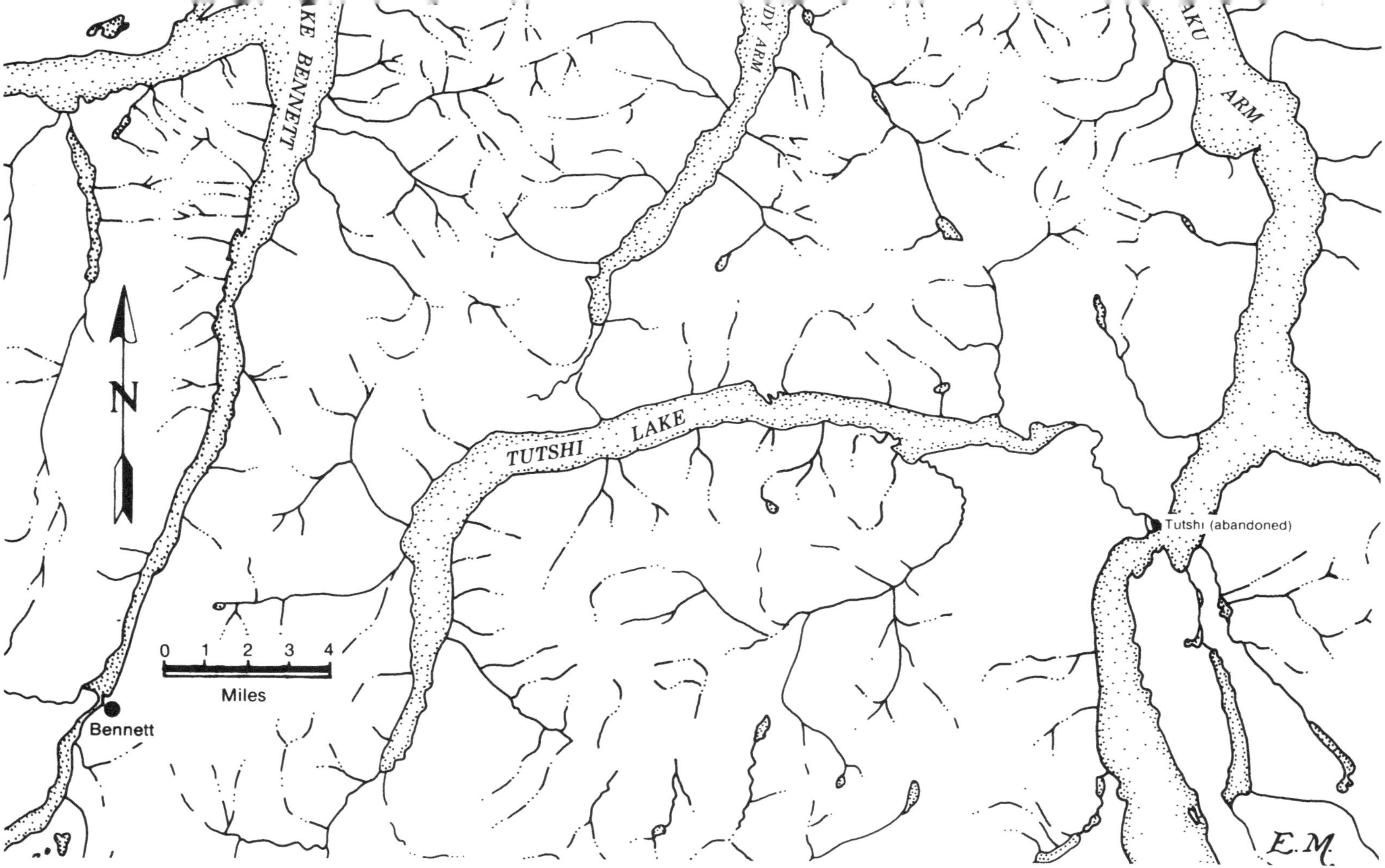

KE BENNETT
DY ARM
AKU ARM
TUTSHI LAKE
Tutshi (abandoned)
N
0 1 2 3 4
Miles
Bennett
E.M.

Clustered around the church are some cabins and shacks used by trappers or migrant squatters laying over in Bennett on their way elsewhere. Those that are in decent shape are usually occupied; the others offer little more shelter than a spruce tree.

On the hilltop behind the church is a cemetery dating back to the gold rush era, and a footpath leads up the stream that connects Lake Bennett and Lake Lindeman; however, it peters out when the going gets rough. The Chilkoot Trail follows the high ground over the rocks between the railroad and the stream, and winds back through the thin timber to Lake Lindeman and up the chain of lakes to the summit.

Just below the church on the lake shore is piling built during the brief steamboat era on the lake. Against the steep bank directly beneath the church is a series of cavities dug out of the sand bank: sites for tents and cabins.

On a clear day, Lake Bennett is one of the most beautiful lakes in the North.

Lake Bennett

Lake Bennett (named by Lt. Schwatka during his trip up there in 1883 for James Gordon Bennett, the publisher of the *New York Herald Tribune* who sponsored the Stanley search in Darkest Africa for Dr. Livingston; I wouldn't presume to guess why Schwatka named it for him though) is some 26 miles (41 km) long with steep mountains jutting up from either side at the southern end. The Bennett Range rises on the west side and a series of peaks on the east side, crowned by Montana Mountain about halfway down the lake.

The southern section of the lake is never more than a mile wide and usually less than a half mile wide, and has all the classic characteristics of a fjord. Camp sites are sparse along this section, except on the east side between the WP&YR tracks and the lake. Camping beside a railroad track leaves much to be desired.

The best campsites are found on the small, low islands that form the boundary between British Columbia and the Yukon. Farther north, beyond the entrance of West Arm, are some campsites on the west side. Use caution crossing the lake near the West Arm entrance due to the strong winds that frequently whip down from the Coast Range.

The scenery along the lake is spectacular with sheer cliffs jutting upward from the water's edge and numerous waterfalls streaming down from melting snowfields above. The lake water is green and the bottom is visible to 10 meters or more below. The wilderness experience is marred only by the presence of the railroad tracks, but some boaters traveling through the sparsely populated North find the tracks and trains reassuring while becoming accustomed to vast open spaces and deep silences.

Perhaps the most spectacular scene on Lake Bennett is when one crosses the open end of West Arm and the row of high, snow-covered peaks of the Coast Range come into view. It gives the lake a sudden, arctic look, quite different from that lent by the lower, barren peaks closer to the lake.

Lake Bennett ends at the small community of Carcross, where a very short, sluggish stream empties Lake Bennett into a small lake named Nares, which in turn feeds into Tagish Lake.

Carcross

Carcross originally was called Caribou Crossing because the woodland caribou (as differentiated from the migratory caribou of the Arctic) used the shallow stream as a crossing. Credited with naming the town is Bishop William Carpenter Bompas, the famous Anglican priest who lived in the Yukon for years before and during the gold rush. It appears that the bishop was fond of abbreviating whenever possible to save himself from writer's cramp, and thus was Carcross born for cartographers.

Carcross has a post office, a hotel with bar and restaurant, a general store, service station and railroad depot. Across the railroad bridge, on the south side of Nares Lake, is the Indian community and cemetery where Skookum Jim, Tagish Charlie and Kate Carmack, George W. Carmack's first wife, were buried.

The most prominent landmarks in Carcross are the steamboat *Tutshi* and the little railroad engine, "The Duchess." As mentioned earlier, the *Tutshi* ran from Carcross down Tagish Lake, Taku Arm and Grahame Inlet to the railroad depot at Taku, where "The Duchess" took over and pulled the cargo and passengers up to Lake Atlin. The *Tutshi* is being restored by the federal and territorial government and is one of only three paddlewheelers left along the river.

There are good campsites near Carcross, the best of which is on the low sand dunes along the shore west of town. However, it is best to camp in the bush due to the incidence of theft in towns (ah, civilization). Other excellent campsites are found down Nares Lake and on the shore of Tagish Lake, only a short paddle from Carcross.

While in Carcross, check your larder for food and fill your tanks with fuel. You will be a day or two, depending on the weather, from the next grocery store and petrol station at Tagish. However, you might want to take side trips down Windy Arm or Taku Arm. It is best to always have a week's supply of food with you. Food and other supplies are available in Carcross.

Nares Lake   Nares Lake, a shallow, narrow lake that more closely resembles a broad, slow river, runs three miles (about five km) between Lake Bennett and Tagish Lake. It is picturesque, with Nares Mountain rising on its north side and Montana Mountain on the south. The shore is wooded with willow, spruce and

After stampeders arrived at the Yukon headwater lakes, they had to build boats for their trip down the river. (Asahel Curtis)

poplar and has several open grassy areas. Most of the best camping sites are on the south shore. On a windy day, Nares usually is very calm and offers a brief respite from fighting the swells of the larger lakes it connects.

Tagish Lake

Tagish Lake runs about 17 miles (27 km) from Nares to the broad stream that connects it to Marsh Lake. About three miles down the lake on the southern side is Windy Arm, a fjord that cuts back into the mountains to terminate beneath Mt. Racine and Mt. Conrad.

It is best to follow the south shore of Tagish Lake across the entrance of Windy Arm. In case of strong winds and wave action you can run with a following instead of cross sea. The best camping sites are along the north shore, which has a series of low, terraced flats with small streams emptying into the lake. After Windy Arm, the scenery opens up considerably and the surrounding mountains take on a gray color.

Just before the entrance of Taku Arm, cross back to the north shore so the south wind will be almost directly on the stern of the boat. Each boater will have to decide on the spot for himself which side is best for his purposes. Usually—but not always—one can see the whitecaps of Windy Arm and Taku Arm a mile or two away, which will give adequate time to switch sides of the lake.

Side Trip Down Windy Arm

Those wishing to explore Windy Arm will be treated to a lake similar in appearance to Lake Bennett sans railroad, with steep mountains rising from near the lake shore. It is 12 miles (19 km) long and limited of camp sites.

About four miles down the lake on the west side is the abandoned town of Conrad, which had hotels, stores, restaurants and churches during the first decade of this century. It was the headquarters of Conrad Consolidated, Ltd., which operated a mine nearby until 1912, when the mine and town were abandoned. A few old buildings including the mine itself remain along with relics of the period.

At the end of Windy Arm is a three-mile-long (five-km) portage trail that leads over to Tutshi Lake, a long, narrow and curving lake some 60 meters higher than the larger lakes around it.

At the risk of being repetitious, you should allow extra time while traveling the lakes to sit out rough weather. More lives have been lost on Tagish Lake where Windy Arm enters than any other place along the lakes or Yukon River.

Tagish Lake North of Taku Arm

As you follow the curve of Tagish Lake around to the north from the entrance of Taku Arm, civilization returns in the form of summer homes built mostly by Whitehorse residents on the north shore. Most are clustered along the broad, shallow stream connecting Tagish and Marsh lakes.

Toward the end of Tagish Lake, the water becomes shallow and moves at about two knots. It offers excellent lake trout fishing.

Tagish

The small town of Tagish is near the end of the stream just before it enters Marsh Lake. A spur of the Alaska Highway, which runs from Jake's Corner to Carcross and up to Whitehorse, crosses the stream at Tagish. Construction of a new

Racine Falls

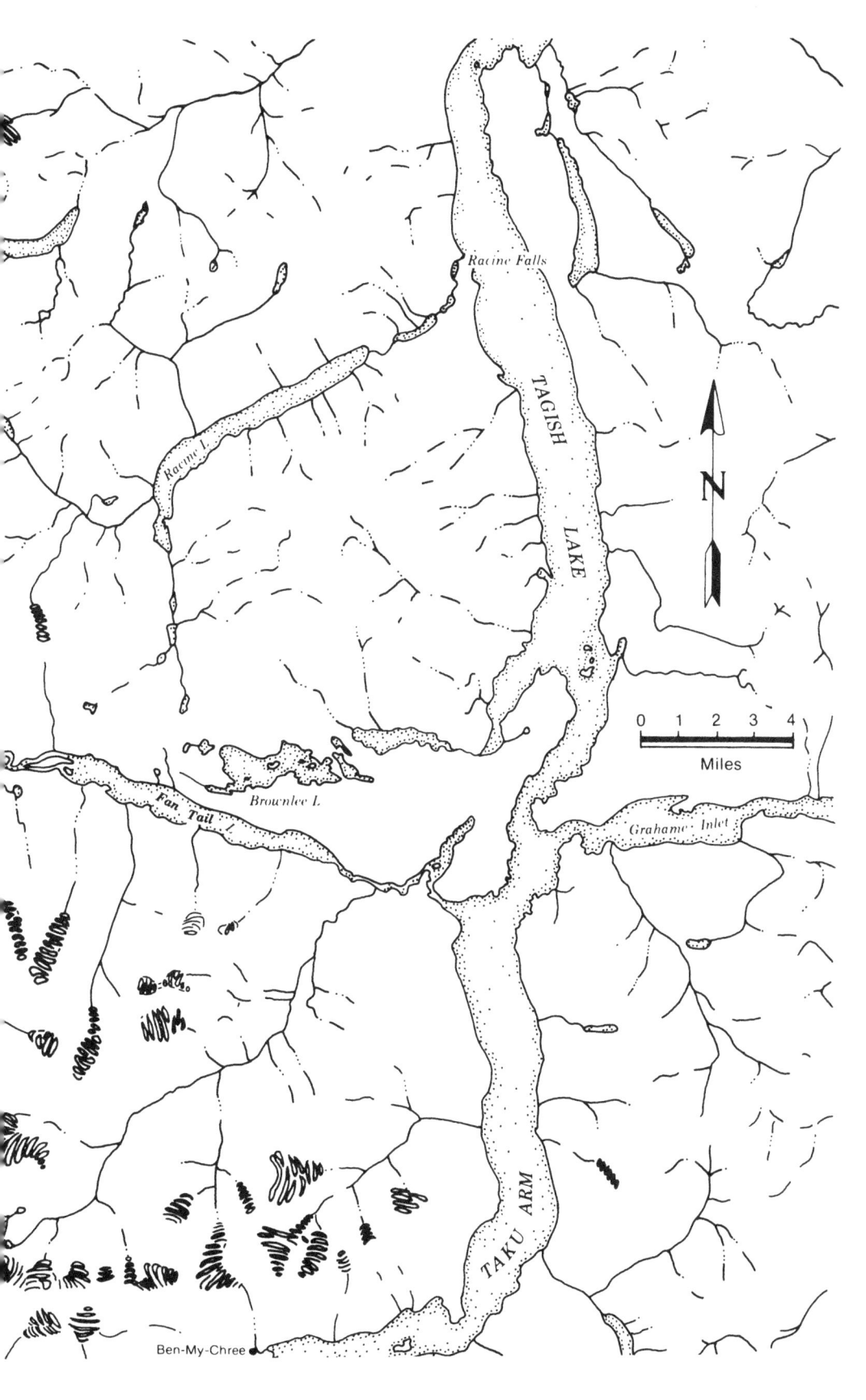

TAGISH LAKE

Racine L.

0 1 2 3 4
Miles

Fan Tail Brownlee L. Grahame Inlet

TAKU ARM

Ben-My-Chree

bridge was scheduled for the summer of 1979, but the activity should not affect passage of boats.

Tagish is the site of the first permanent establishment of the Mounties, who set up a post there to collect customs and serve as a checkpoint for stampeders en route to the Klondike. Before that, the Tagish band of Indians had camps there because of the good fishing and hunting nearby.

There is a territorial park on the east side just upstream from the bridge. Tagish has grocery stores and service stations, a Mountie post and numerous permanent and summer homes. On the west side of the bridge and down the road about 90 meters is a grocery store with a good selection of staples, gifts and tourist items. Unfortunately, the long-popular landmark bakery at this bridge has now closed.

Camping at Tagish is limited to the unimproved territorial campground near the bridge, but good campsites can be found on Marsh Lake.

Today visitors can traverse White Pass in comfort on the White Pass & Yukon Route, which runs between Skagway and Whitehorse.

Headwaters
—Atlin to Tagish

Many believe that Lake Atlin and the small town of Atlin is the most beautiful place in the North, an opinion difficult to fault. The lake is the largest natural lake in British Columbia; it is 66 miles (106 km) long and from 2 to 3 miles (3 to 5 km) wide. It is studded with islands ranging from tiny rocks to the vast Teresa Island with Birch Mountain. The view across the lake from the town of Atlin is one of the most impressive anywhere in the world. Atlin Mountain rises majestically from the lake and one never tires of watching the play of sunlight on its summit and ridges. A rock glacier flows slowly, steadily from a cirque high up on its face, and the view across to it is accented with the small islands between.

Atlin

The town of Atlin has an easy-going charm, which is being preserved by the new people moving there—many migrating from the United States—who want to keep the casual life of semi-isolation. Atlin is 61 miles (98 km) south from Johnson's Crossing, an intersection on the Alaska Highway, over a gravel road. Atlin is 110 miles (177 km) from Whitehorse. Since the road ends at Atlin, it is not one of those places travelers see on their way to somewhere else; they must be headed for Atlin if they are going to see it.

The visitor to the town should plan on extra time to drive out to the ghost town of Surprise at the head of Surprise Lake a few miles east of town. Old gold mining operations and abandoned dredges are scattered along Pine Creek, and a few miners still work and rework the old claims.

An ideal way to see the chain of lakes from Atlin (Lake Atlin, Grahame Inlet, Taku Arm and out to Tagish and Marsh to intersect with the route just described) is to rent a canoe in Whitehorse, arrange for its transportation to Atlin, and then follow this route back to Whitehorse. This makes an excellent trip for a two-week vacation. Since the lakes are so vast, many prefer using canoes or boats with motors.

Lake Atlin The shore of Lake Atlin is virtually deserted today, and only a handful of trappers' cabins can be seen along the route. After you leave sight of the town, it is unlikely another boat will be seen, unless it is the jet boat used to take people up and down the lake on sightseeing trips and deliver provisions to the few living on the lakes.

For the boater planning to see the highlights of Lake Atlin, then head for the other lakes, this itinerary is recommended:

Cross the lake from Atlin and follow Torres Channel between the west shore and Teresa Island. The open lake can become very rough and the western shore is the more beautiful. This route takes you past the foot of Atlin Mountain and down the narrow Torres Channel with protection from the wind.

The best campsites are found at the southern end of Teresa Island and on the small islands south of it, such as Copper Island. There are numerous bays and inlets that can confuse you while seeking a passage through to the open lake, and it is best to ask for landmarks from townspeople before leaving.

Early in the summer you can see moose cows and their calves on the islands, where the cows keep them for protection from predators. For their protection—and yours—do not approach them or otherwise disturb the quiet they need.

There are innumerable campsites along the islands and the lake water is clear, cold and pure. Don't hesitate to dip into it for drinking water. The only problem with choosing a campsite is selecting the best of so many choices. Some of the most protected campsites are on the northern side of Copper Island in what is known locally as First Passage (the first route from the north between the islands back to the open lake). Second Passage is a wider body of water and more exposed to wind on the shore. These islands offer excellent hiking along the beaches, and most have established trails made by the moose while they nurse their calves during summer months. It is best to make enough

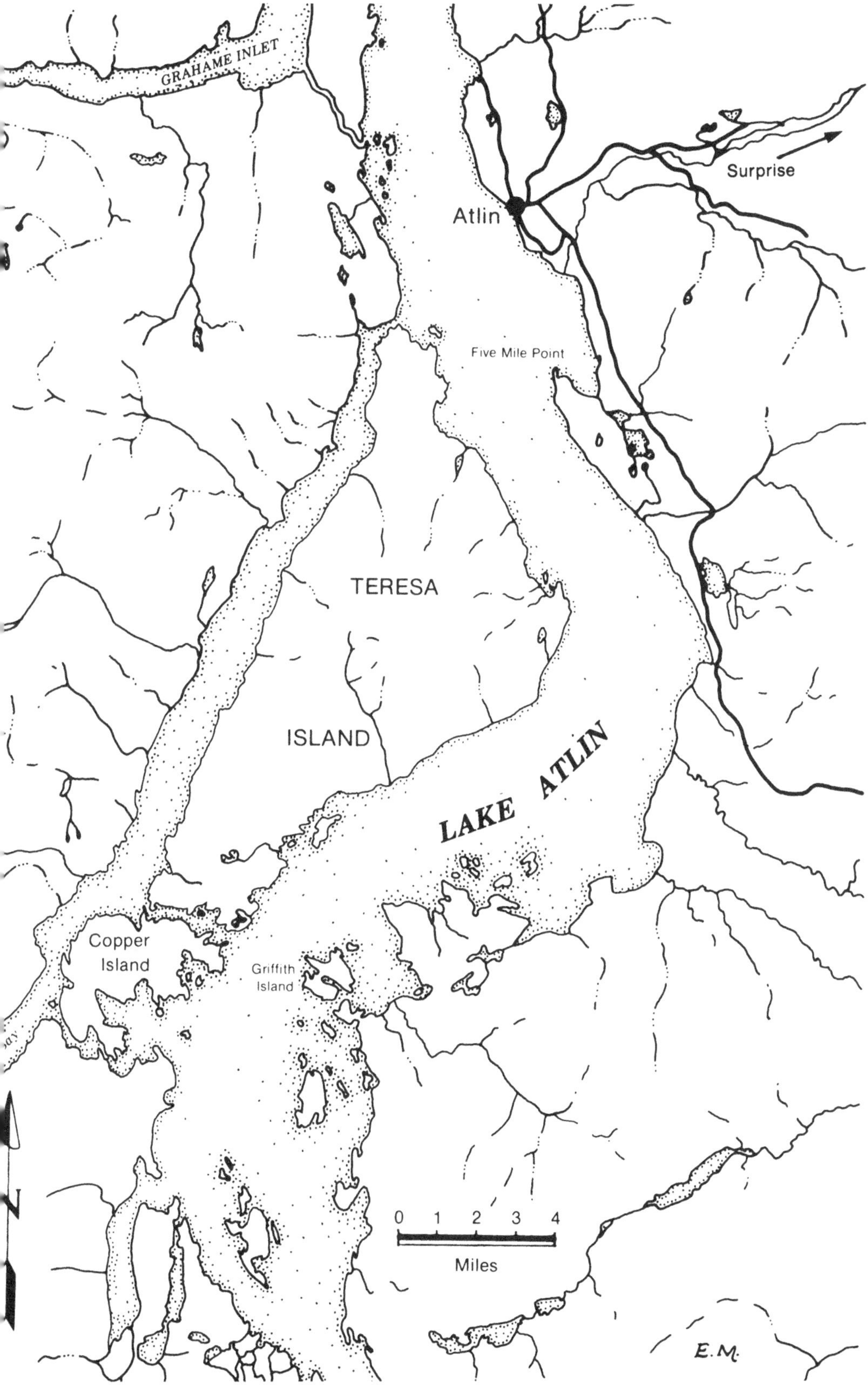
GRAHAME INLET
Atlin
Surprise
Five Mile Point
TERESA
ISLAND
LAKE ATLIN
Copper
Island
Griffith
Island
0 1 2 3 4
Miles
E.M.

noise to let them know you are near (which is not the same thing as being raucous), and to watch them from the beach.

The following day, if the weather is calm, you can go on down the lake to Llewellyn Inlet and hike to the glacier. Since there are several unpredictable factors involved in traveling on such a large body of water, it's best to break camp and carry everything with you rather than leave your gear at the first night's camp. You might be raided by a curious, hungry bear; you could become marooned by a storm; you might want to stay at Llewellyn longer and camp there. Worst of all, you might forget your landmarks and spend hours looking for your portable home.

Llewellyn Inlet curves around a point, then heads straight back to the Coast Range and Juneau Icecap between sheer cliffs on either side. The trail to the glacier begins at a gravel beach to the west of Llewellyn River, and the trailhead is protected from the wind.

The trail is named the Stewart James Trail in honor of the late Mr. James who led people to Llewellyn Glacier. The short trail heads up through the gnarled and wind-twisted timber, over boulders and down to the moraine plain where the glacier has receded. By crossing the stream at a shallow spot, you can walk all the way to the glacier's snout, which stretches for more than a mile across the valley floor.

A shorter route follows the stream on the west side to an outcropping of rocks that gives a high, overall view of the glacier and mountains behind. At your feet is a clear stream emptying into the glacier milk river that creates a green ribbon in the white river as they merge.

The trailhead is an excellent place to camp in case of heavy winds that can sweep down from the icecap in the afternoon and evening. Generally, the early mornings are calm and you can get out of the inlet and back into the protection of the islands before the heavy winds return. It is worth noting here that the deepest spot measured in Lake Atlin is 244 meters, at the head of Llewellyn Inlet.

Local boaters recommend staying with the west shore, but the choice is obviously the individual boater's. If it bothers you to retrace a route, remember that you see things from a different perspective when doing so. Also, the west side of the lake is spectacular.

A young girl ties up a canoe at the head of the Stewart James Trail at the south end of Lake Atlin.

Atlin River

After returning to Atlin, you should reprovision because it is the last chance until Tagish, which is more than 80 miles (130 km) by a direct route and about 120 miles (193 km) if you make all the recommended side trips.

It is recommended that you hire a guide in Atlin to help you down the Atlin River. The three-kilometer-long river drops 15 meters and runs at about 9 knots; it is filled with rapids, boulders, backwashes and shallows. It is very dangerous for canoes and kayaks, less so for larger boats. It is best run in late June or early July before the highwater period in late summer, when the force of the current literally stands the river on its edge in a few places.

The river begins at Scotia Bay, across the lake to the northwest from Atlin. There are remains of the WP&YR railroad depot and rail-less ties leading back into the timber. Just below the head of the river are some old, rickety platforms out over the river, which were used by sports fishermen when the railroad was in operation.

Llewellyn Glacier as seen from a ridge near Lake Atlin.

Atlin River is difficult to scout from the bank because the railroad bed does not follow the bank closely. It involves a great deal of brush beating to study the stream before taking it on. When the water is lower in the early summer, the main danger is hitting rocks just below the surface.

About the only method of scouting it first is to arrange to ride in the jet boat from Atlin on a run down to Grahame Inlet or beyond. The boat runs at a high speed to stay off the bottom, and you have to be quick of eye.

Obviously, many boats and canoes have run the river with absolute safety, and this is not intended to scare everyone away from it. But it is meant to encourage caution. There have been drownings on the river, some by experienced whitewater kayakers and canoeists.

When the river empties into Grahame Inlet, the safest route is to run on out into the inlet a few hundred feet to avoid the shallow bottom, then swing back around to the railroad station at Taku, where there are sheltered places to tie up out of the wind.

Taku is privately owned now, but the owner generously permits camping with the plea to leave the area clean. It is an interesting place to camp and poke around the old buildings and railroad shops. The waiting room still has the benches for passengers' convenience and there are numerous tools and pieces of railroad equipment scattered around. The dock is sagging, but still has three narrow-gauge flatcars parked there that were too heavy or expensive to transport out when the steamboats stopped running. Offshore a few feet is the hulk of a steamboat resting on the shallow bottom, and back up in the brush are several small cabins in which railroad workers lived. Some still have furniture in them, but vandals have done their duty and torn much of the furniture into debris.

There is excellent grayling fishing at the river mouth and Grahame Inlet is noted for its lake trout fishing. You can easily spend an extra day at Taku fishing along the lake shore or hiking up the old railroad right-of-way, trying to imagine the area thirty years ago.

Two miles (three km) down the inlet from Taku is an abandoned sawmill with a group of cabins and machine sheds in good condition. A hunting guide uses the cabins in the autumn,

Taku

which probably accounts for their good condition. Outside are numerous saw blades, a steam plant, belts, and several piles of rough-sawn lumber left unsold or undelivered when the mill closed. It was built in part to cut ties for the Taku-to-Scotia Bay railroad, but also provided lumber for home building and other uses in the area.

Grahame Inlet
Grahame Inlet runs 16 miles (26 km) from Taku to Golden Gate, where it enters Taku Arm. A few homes have been built along its shores, mostly summer residences, with the exception of the residence and rental cabins a mile east of the mouth of the inlet on the south side. The proprietors are reservoirs of knowledge on the north, and a visit with them is comparable to a seminar on the subject.

Golden Gate
Just west of the cabins is Golden Gate, the entrance to Taku Arm. The entrance received its name for the brilliant fall colors in the area and the marvelous view of the mountains that opens up as one enters Taku Arm.

Like the other long, narrow lakes of this area, Taku Arm is noted for its heavy swells. It is recommended that you head directly across the arm from Golden Gate, then follow the west shore to the south. Then, when the arm swings sharply to the west toward Ben-My-Chree, cut across to the opposite (south) side, and follow that shore on to the end. The return trip with a following sea can be made on the eastern shore to see both sides of the arm and the old mine and town over there.

Taku Arm offers very few campsites along either shore because it is rocky and hemmed in by steep mountains on both sides. By following the shoreline closely, an occasional smooth beach can be found among the rocks. (The author knows from bitter-cold experience. We were wet and cold and couldn't find a place to land on the rocky shore. At last we found one of the small beaches by a trapper's cabin. Then the sun came out and the clouds parted.)

Taku Arm, South from Golden Gate

Due to the unpredictable weather, many boaters do not explore the southern half of Taku Arm, below Golden Gate. But the trip is worth whatever discomfort may result. When you reach the final curve in the arm and the Florence Range stands up directly above the icy water, sheer as a canyon wall to more than 2100 meters, the spectacular view is one that is not duplicated anywhere else in the area.

If you cannot continue on to the end of the arm, a small, rocky island near the south shore has good campsites sheltered from the wind and good beaches for tying up the boat away from the waves. Here, you can pitch a tent with a view out to the stunning Florence Range and watch the midnight sun manipulate the colors of the rock walls and the snow on top.

Ben-My-Chree

At the very tip of the arm is a long, rickety pier sticking out over the mudflats from the glacial silt. This is the entrance to the charming ghost town of Ben-My-Chree. To avoid having to play steeplejack and climb up to the dock, follow the shallow stream on the right (north) side along the cliff and beach the boat beneath the pier.

Ben-My-Chree began its colorful history as a mine up in the hills above the buildings. Unfortunately, the mine collapsed and the owners never reopened it. Instead, they began importing plants and trees from all over the world and turned the place into a garden. The owners of the mine, Mr. and Mrs. Otto Partridge, came from the Isle of Man and named the place, which in Manx (the Isle of Man language) means "girl of my heart."

Previously, he had operated a sawmill on Lake Bennett, then was associated with a group that ran small sternwheelers on the lakes under the corporate name of Bennett Lake & Klondike Navigation Co.

After Ben-My-Chree became a garden spot in a hostile climate, the steamboats that ran from Carcross to Taku began stopping there regularly. Passengers tramped down the long pier and along a trail that led between pine, fir and numerous kinds of shrubs. They were served tea and cakes and rhubarb wine, and were free to stroll out among the formal gardens and sit in a gazebo with a small, cold stream running through it.

After the Partridges died six months apart in 1930 and 1931, the transportation company, WP&YR, continued operating the garden spot until 1955, when they retired the *Tutshi* at Carcross.

Due to its isolated location, Ben-My-Chree has not suffered the ravages of vandalism to the extent of other stops along this route. The buildings are still in relatively good shape; the furnishings are intact. In one building is a bulletin board with several hundred business cards thumbtacked there over the years by visitors.

Part of the pier has sagged down to the mudflat, but the whimsical statues, including a gigantic wooden mosquito and a dwarf prehistoric monster, still stand in the yard.

The next stop of interest on the return trip is at the Engineer gold mine on the east shore about 10 miles (16 km) from Golden Gate. It is one of those common stories among mining circles of a site that had the gold, but never quite enough. It received its name from the fact that a group of engineers working for WP&YR discovered it and began operating it in 1899. It was sold in 1907, idled by litigation, and opened again in 1924.

The Engineer Gold Mine on Taku Arm is silent now, but there are always rumors that it will start up again.

In 1930, a power dam was built on the Wann River, a bit south of the mine, barely in time for the mine owners to run out of operating capital and close it again. The mine has not been in operation since, but there are always rumors that this or that group is going to open it.

A trail leads from the mine back down the lakeshore to the power dam, now gone, but a cluster of buildings still stands. Some are owned by summer residents. The mine building runs up the hillside and shows evidence of numerous additions as the mine was enlarged. Most of the machinery is still inside, and a number of old, rotting ore sacks lie about with EGM stenciled on them.

Taku Arm, North from Golden Gate

As Taku Arm runs past Golden Gate, it narrows somewhat, and islands of various sizes are scattered around. Campsites are abundant north of Golden Gate, and most boaters select one near a stream entering the lake because it is easier to catch grayling at a stream's entrance. The west shore is steeper and less marshy than the east side. You will probably want to stay on the west side because there will be fewer mosquitos than in the marshy areas. One of the few places you have to watch the bottom is near the entrance of Deep Bay, where islands stand in the middle of the lake. Pinnacles lead from the shore to the islands; some are below the surface and can be seen easily in the clear water.

The beauty along upper Taku Arm is so constant, yet changing, that it is easy to take it for granted. It is not the rugged, spectacular beauty of the lower end, nor the Switzerland-type of scenery around Atlin. Rather it is a subtle beauty with modest mountains undulating into the distance and thick forests of spruce and willow interlaced by small streams and game trails. On a calm day the mountains and trees reflect themselves perfectly in the water and the color of the water turns the reflected sky into a deeper blue-green with the clouds standing out in bold relief. It is like looking into a sky through polarized glasses.

One of the several side hikes available from the lake—perhaps the best—is up Racine River to Racine Lake. The river ends with a big noise as it tumbles down to form Racine Falls less than 60 meters from the lake. A trail leads up from an old dock to a viewpoint directly in front of the falls, where spray washes over you as you watch the different shapes the water takes in its tumble. The trail winds through beaver-thinned forests to the lake and across a flume dug years ago for a power-project that has been long abandoned.

Other side hikes can be made on old trails to Fan Tail Lake and Tutshi Lake. These are not maintained and are grown over except where animals have kept them open, so be prepared for some brush-beating.

Tagish Lake As Taku Arm nears Tagish Lake, the mountains gradually flatten out and become gray and barren. There is virtually no vegetation growing on them, and the forest runs to their bases and suddenly stops. These low, granite mountains are characteristic of the Tagish to Lake Laberge area: no high mountains are seen again until the section of river below Laberge.

The course of the trip from here on, through Tagish Lake and on to Tagish, is the same course as that described in the previous chapter on Lake Bennett. The description is repeated here for convenience's sake:

Tagish Lake North of Taku Arm

As you follow the curve of Tagish Lake around to the north from the entrance of Taku Arm, civilization returns in the form of summer homes built mostly by Whitehorse residents on the north shore. Most are clustered along the broad, shallow stream connecting Tagish and Marsh lakes.

Toward the end of Tagish Lake, the water becomes shallow and moves at about two knots. It offers excellent lake trout fishing.

Tagish

The small town of Tagish is near the end of the stream just before it enters Marsh Lake. A spur of the Alaska Highway, which runs from Jake's Corner to Carcross and up to Whitehorse, crosses the stream at Tagish. There are usually so many people fishing from the bridge that you have to be careful to avoid getting tangled in the lines.

Racine Falls is only a few feet west of Taku Arm. This short side hike is one of the nicest choices from Taku Arm.

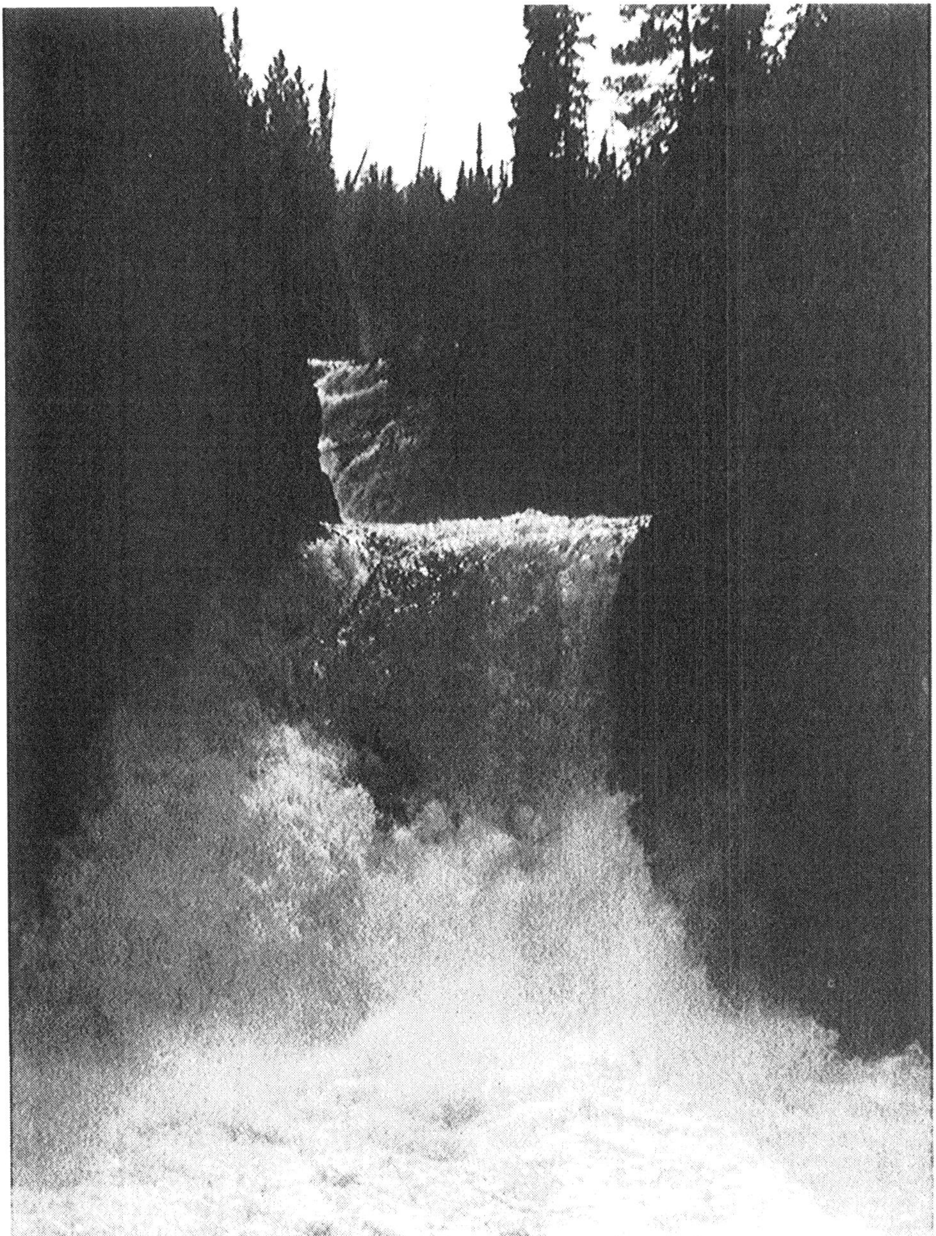

Marsh Lake to Whitehorse

Marsh Lake begins just below the town of Tagish. It is a shallow, warm, 20-mile-long (32-km) body of water, only 2 miles (3 km) wide, that is the last in the chain of headwater lakes before the Yukon River.

Marsh Lake is sneered at by wilderness buffs because the Alaska Highway runs along its east shore and houses are frequent along that side. It is something of the ugly duckling of the headwater system and more often spoken of as an inconvenience than a place of beauty.

The lake isn't as ugly as the chroniclers would have us believe. It has a subdued beauty of its own, though, and by following the west shore, the noise and dust and signs of population are avoided. There are good campsites on the shore, especially at Sand Point, a peninsula of sand protruding out into the lake with a sheltered cove on the north side.

Don't be surprised if you see water skiers on the lake near the northern end where the settlement of M'Clintock has grown up. The shallow water is warmer than the other lakes, and in warm weather the hardy can be seen criss-crossing their wakes with a minimum of goosepimples.

A few kilometers before the Yukon River begins below Marsh Lake, you will see the first evidences of two characteristics common to the river all along its course. On the west bank of Marsh Lake you will see high banks undercut by the water and sliding off into the lake. These are called cutbanks in the North. In the same general area spruce trees are undercut by the water, and they hang crazily out into the water before their roots finally give way and they are washed out of the lake and into the river. These are called sweepers since they can sweep your hat off—or you out of a boat—as you pass them. They also "sweep" the water before giving way.

These characteristics serve as an introduction to the river itself. No great efforts have been made to channel the river through the use of dikes or other methods.

Source of the Yukon

There is lingering discussion of where the Yukon River begins. No monument exists stating that the Yukon headwaters spring from any particular spot. (The Columbia River is easier to track.)

But the Yukon has grown in length, thanks to the renaming of the streams above Fort Selkirk. When Robert Campbell established Fort Selkirk at the confluence of the Yukon and the Pelly (which he named), he called the main stream above Selkirk the Lewes River. The 30-mile segment from Hootalinqua, where the Teslin River enters, back to Lake Laberge, was the Thirtymile River. In time, the Yukon designation moved back up to Hootalinqua and, later, beyond Lake Laberge to Marsh Lake.

Many maps still in use show the Lewes River flowing past Whitehorse, and call the portion from Lake Laberge to Hootalinqua the Thirtymile, or Old Thirtymile, River—perhaps because that stretch of river is so beautiful it deserves distinction.

The River Begins

From Marsh Lake, the river meanders through low, marshy spots before flowing beneath a bridge for the Alaska Highway, then into the small lake behind the dam at the highway crossing. There are numerous sloughs and islands along this stretch of river and it is easy to wander out of the main current into the still backwaters.

The dam is known locally as the Marsh Lake Dam although it is not at the lake. It was built to help the steamboats begin running early in the summer each year by flushing the ice out of the river below Whitehorse, and out of Lake Laberge. Now it is used as part of the flood control system and to adjust the level of Schwatka Lake behind the hydroelectric dam at Whitehorse.

A self-operating lock at the right (east) side of the dam will hold four or five small boats at a time. It has simple instructions and requires no special education to operate. The drop is from one to three meters, depending on the water level. When leaving the lock, paddle directly out into the main current to avoid a back eddy directly ahead.

For the next 6 miles/10 kilometers, the river meanders gracefully through dense undergrowth and past cutbanks and sweepers. The river gradually narrows, then swings through a wide valley only to become enclosed again. It winds around several S-turns; paddlers will appreciate this stretch since steering is the only exercise required.

About one kilometer above Miles Canyon is a sign identifying a flat area covered with dense vegetation as Canyon City. Little of the townsite is left except some rotten logs, but during the stampede to the Klondike and before the WP&YR rail line was completed to Whitehorse, it was an important town. Canyon City is the last place boats can be taken out of the river with ease before entering Miles Canyon.

Canyon City

Even though the canyon has been partially tamed by the Whitehorse dam, the speed of the river is noticeably faster the closer you get to the canyon. Before the dam was built, the water was ferocious for a five-mile (eight-km) stretch. It was compressed into such a small space that it crested about a meter high in the center, created two whirlpools at the end of the canyon, then dropped down into Whitehorse Rapids, which had high stands of water that looked like galloping white horses with manes flying. It still wasn't through. Just below Whitehorse Rapids was another set called Squaw Rapids with boulders poking ominously above the surface.

Miles Canyon

Some of the early arrivals tried running the canyon and rapids with only limited success. Several stampeders were drowned and many others lost all their gear after hauling it over the passes the previous winter. That changed when the Mounties' honcho, the famous Sam Steele, arrived. In his direct, no-nonsense and infinitely wise fashion, he laid down the law of the canyon:

> No women or children were permitted to run the rapids; no boats would go through until the Mounties determined they were safe; no boat with people in them unless the Mounties were sure they were manned by competent men. Violators would be fined $100.

Some men hired on as guides through the canyon and rapids, under the approving eye of the Mounties. (There is nothing to the story that Jack London made a small fortune as a Miles Canyon guide. He and his partners shot the rapids and barely made it through Lake Laberge before freezeup in 1897 and wintered on the Stewart River.)

Miles Canyon is only a shadow of its former self now that a hydroelectric dam downstream slows the river's speed through the canyon. (Yukon Government photo)

Most stampeders hauled their boats to the bank at Canyon City and began the tiresome business of portaging their gear five miles (eight km) over the rugged terrain to where Whitehorse now stands, then lined their boats through the canyon and over the rapids.

However, an enterprising man named Norman Maculay had a better idea. He built a wooden-railed tramway from Canyon City over the hills to the foot of the rapids, bought some horses and made a small fortune at $25 a boatload.

The canyon and rapids were transportation barriers between the upper lakes and the river. Steamboats built at Lake Bennett for the gold rush went down the river through the canyon and never returned; no boat was powerful enough to go back upstream.

Thus, the city of Whitehorse was born where the railroad ended and the river navigation began.

Today, running Miles Canyon presents little difficulty. There is only a hint of the whirlpools and the crest in the center has been flattened out by the backwaters of the dam. A white footbridge spans the 15-meter canyon and as you pass through it you can see hundreds of swallow nests stuck to the basalt walls. The bridge was built in 1922 for the visit of a Governor-General of Canada, the Queen's representative. It was named the Robert Lowe Bridge for an early territorial councillor, and was the first bridge across the Yukon River anywhere along its length.

Schwatka Lake

After going through the canyon, you immediately enter Schwatka Lake, named for the American army officer who led an expedition over the passes and down the Yukon River in 1883 and presented several geographical features with names that stuck, among them Miles Canyon in honor of his commanding officer, Brig. Gen. Nelson A. Miles of Vancouver Barracks, Washington.

At the end of the lake, just above the dam, is a government dock used by both boats and seaplanes. Here you can dock and arrange for transportation around the dam. If you have rented canoes in Whitehorse, the rental agency will take care of the portage, and local taxicab companies can haul other smaller boats around, such as canoes and kayaks.

This 1898 scene shows stampeders running Whitehorse Rapids, yet another obstacle on the way to the gold fields. At the time, these rapids were, if anything, worse than Miles Canyon. (Asahel Curtis)

During winter months, Whitehorse Rapids was so clogged with jumbled blocks of ice that nobody could use the river as a route to anywhere. (Asahel Curtis)

Whitehorse

You have arrived in Whitehorse, the largest city to be encountered on the trip, and the place to stock up for the river ahead. It is best to buy *everything* you'll need for the rest of the trip here and replenish only perishables and fuel at Carmacks, 200 miles (322 km) downstream.

Do not leave your equipment unattended here. Theft and vandalism have become major problems in the cities and along the highways of the North.

Whitehorse is the capital of the Yukon and its largest city, with some 12,000 residents, or more than half the total Yukon population. It has all the conveniences of home: department stores, fast-food places, a coin-operated laundromat, several hotels, restaurants—the works.

mile 0

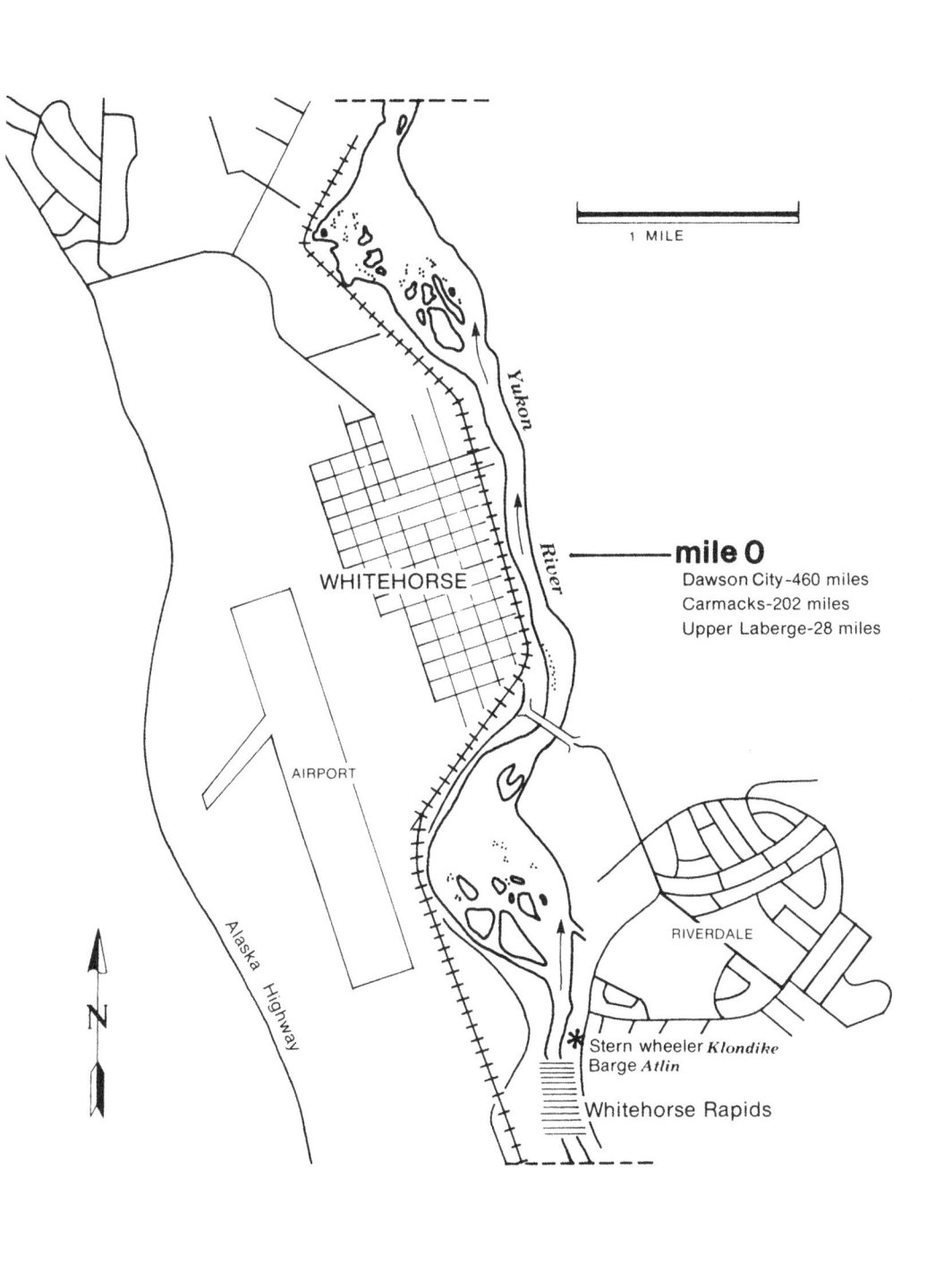

mile 0
Dawson City - 460 miles
Carmacks - 202 miles
Upper Laberge - 28 miles

WHITEHORSE

AIRPORT

Alaska Highway

Yukon River

RIVERDALE

* Stern wheeler *Klondike*
Barge *Atlin*

Whitehorse Rapids

1 MILE

N

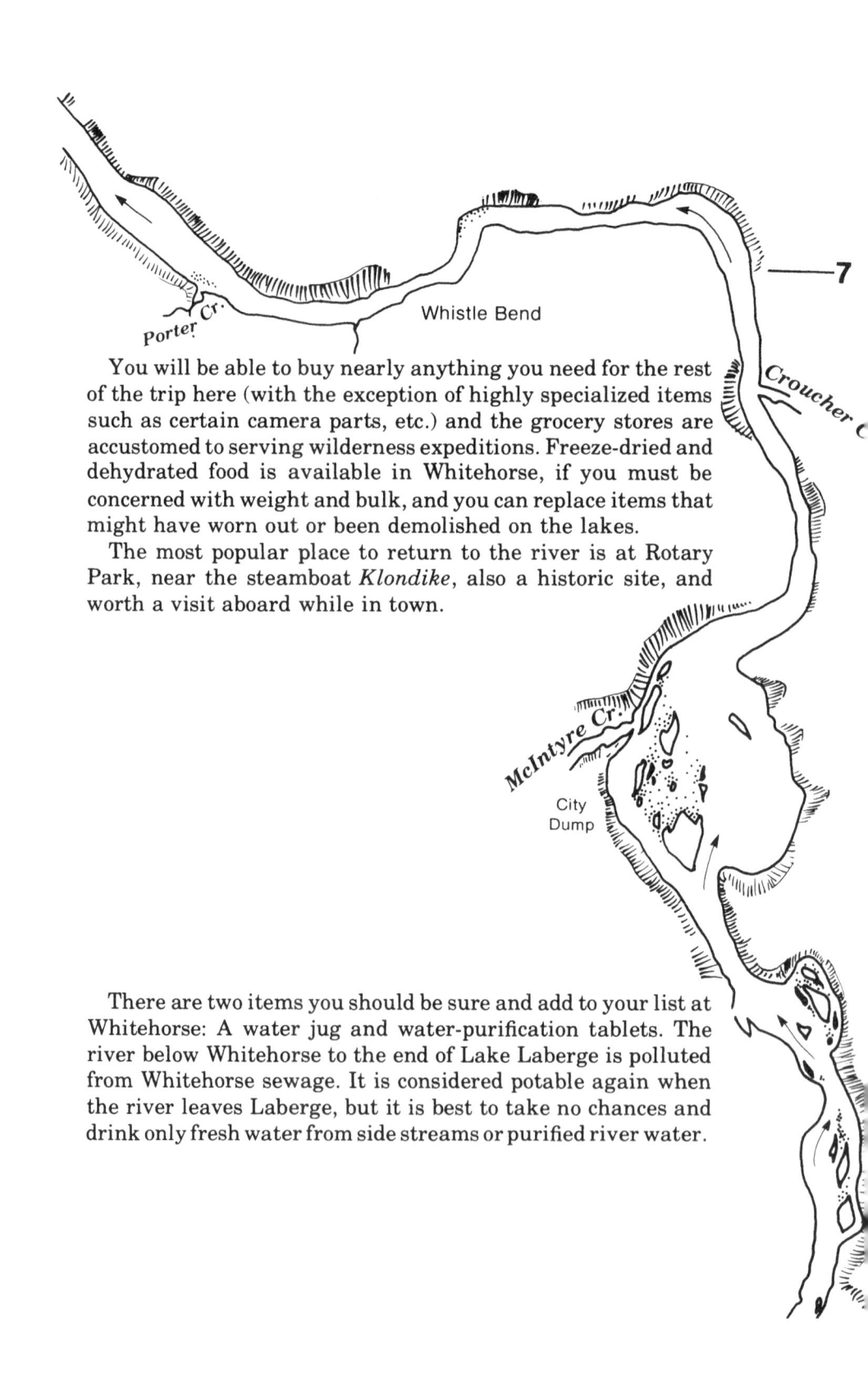

You will be able to buy nearly anything you need for the rest of the trip here (with the exception of highly specialized items such as certain camera parts, etc.) and the grocery stores are accustomed to serving wilderness expeditions. Freeze-dried and dehydrated food is available in Whitehorse, if you must be concerned with weight and bulk, and you can replace items that might have worn out or been demolished on the lakes.

The most popular place to return to the river is at Rotary Park, near the steamboat *Klondike*, also a historic site, and worth a visit aboard while in town.

There are two items you should be sure and add to your list at Whitehorse: A water jug and water-purification tablets. The river below Whitehorse to the end of Lake Laberge is polluted from Whitehorse sewage. It is considered potable again when the river leaves Laberge, but it is best to take no chances and drink only fresh water from side streams or purified river water.

A view to the north from the top of Richtofen Island, which is noted for its variety of wild flowers in early summer.

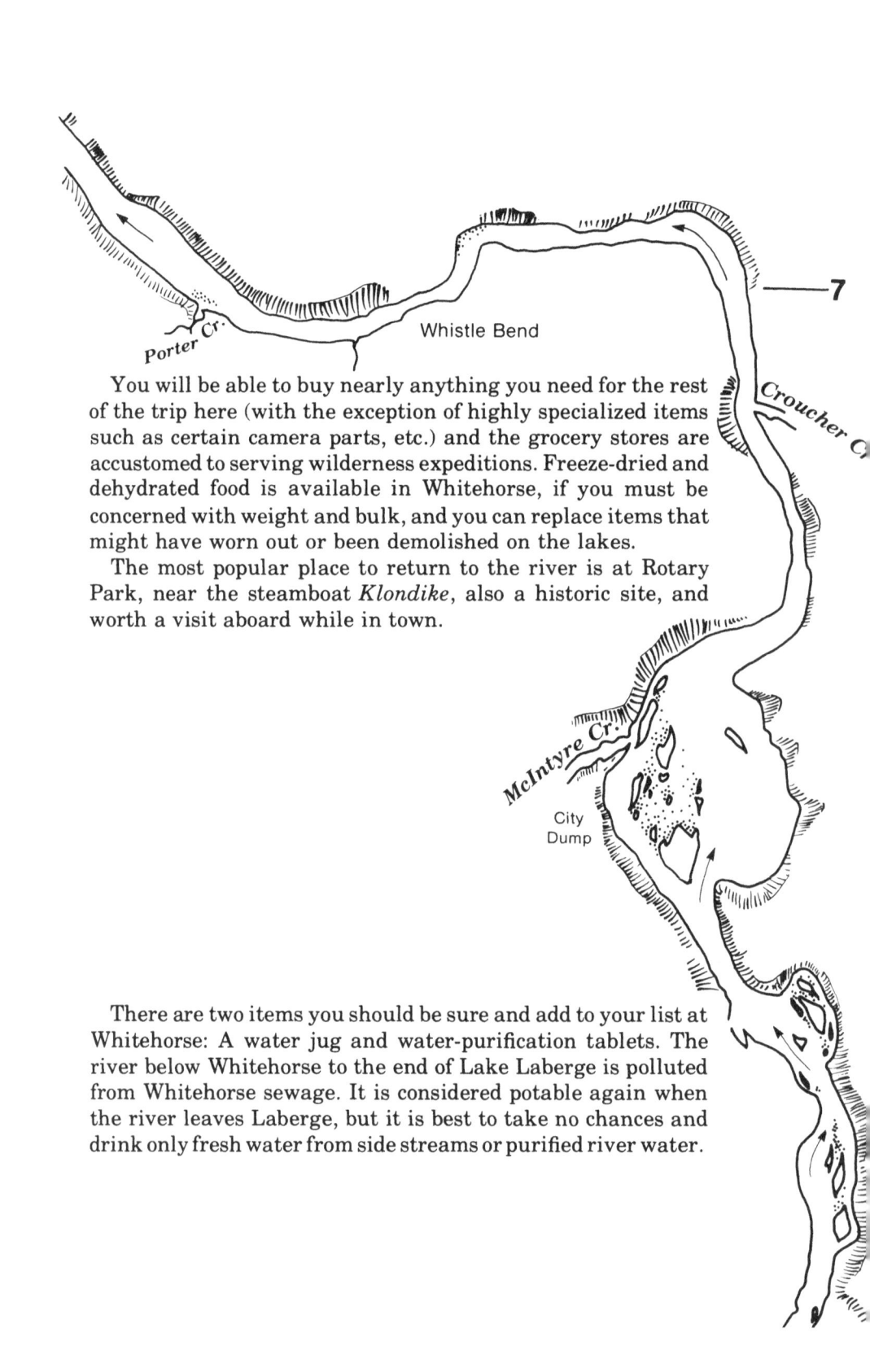

You will be able to buy nearly anything you need for the rest of the trip here (with the exception of highly specialized items such as certain camera parts, etc.) and the grocery stores are accustomed to serving wilderness expeditions. Freeze-dried and dehydrated food is available in Whitehorse, if you must be concerned with weight and bulk, and you can replace items that might have worn out or been demolished on the lakes.

The most popular place to return to the river is at Rotary Park, near the steamboat *Klondike*, also a historic site, and worth a visit aboard while in town.

There are two items you should be sure and add to your list at Whitehorse: A water jug and water-purification tablets. The river below Whitehorse to the end of Lake Laberge is polluted from Whitehorse sewage. It is considered potable again when the river leaves Laberge, but it is best to take no chances and drink only fresh water from side streams or purified river water.

Whitehorse to Hootalinqua

The river widens after leaving Whitehorse and soon becomes more than 400 meters wide. The banks are low for the first few miles, then gradually rise to nearly 60 meters high in places.

The Yukon picks up both speed and width after the Takhini River enters. A short distance below the Takhini's entrance is a vast burned-off area, evidence of the big forest fire of 1954 when Whitehorse was threatened. The area is covered now with the beautiful purple fireweed as the forest struggles against the harsh climate and thin topsoil to return.

Takhini River mile 15

There are numerous places to camp along this section of the river, but unless one camps at the Takhini River entrance where unpolluted water is available, it is best to continue to Lake Laberge.

The river slows noticeably as it nears Lake Laberge and mudflats become more evident. To the right of the lake entrance is a low, grassy bank called Scow Point above rows of piling stubs where pile dikes were built to control the channel during the steamboat era. By following the lake around to the right, you can find an adequate campsite among a group of abandoned buildings beside Laberge Creek. At departure, however, it is wise for the sake of safety from the storms to swing back to the left side and follow the west shore all the way down the lake. Most weather comes from the west out of the Pacific and the St. Elias Range, although storms, often crackling thunderstorms, blow in from the other directions.

Lake Laberge mile 28

A government campground is opposite Richtofen Island. You can either camp there with the motorized campers, or merely load up on fresh water at the campground and go over to the island to camp or continue down the lake. There are some beautiful campsites along the east shore of the high-backed

15

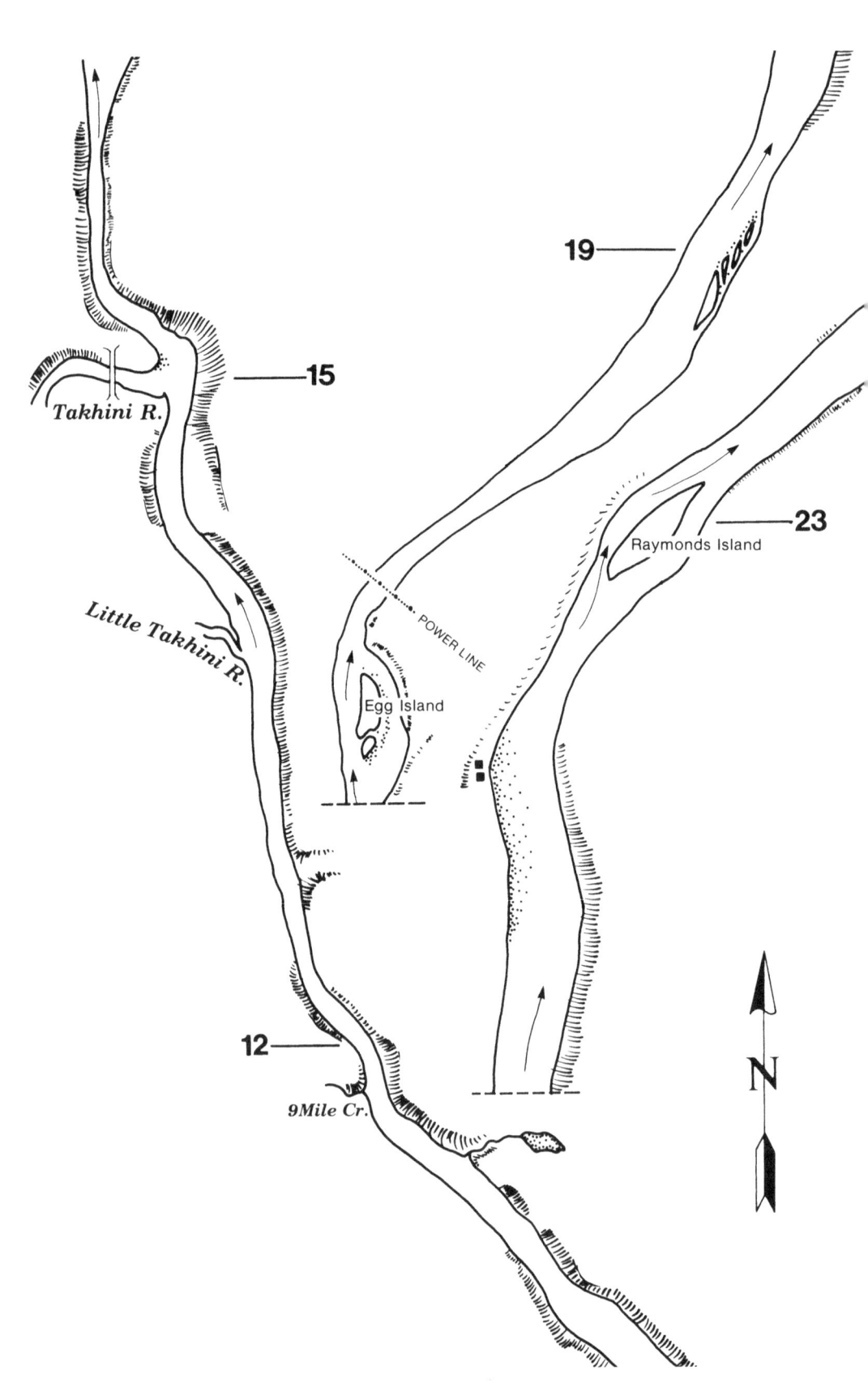

19

Takhini R.

23

Raymonds Island

Little Takhini R.

POWER LINE

Egg Island

12

9 Mile Cr.

N

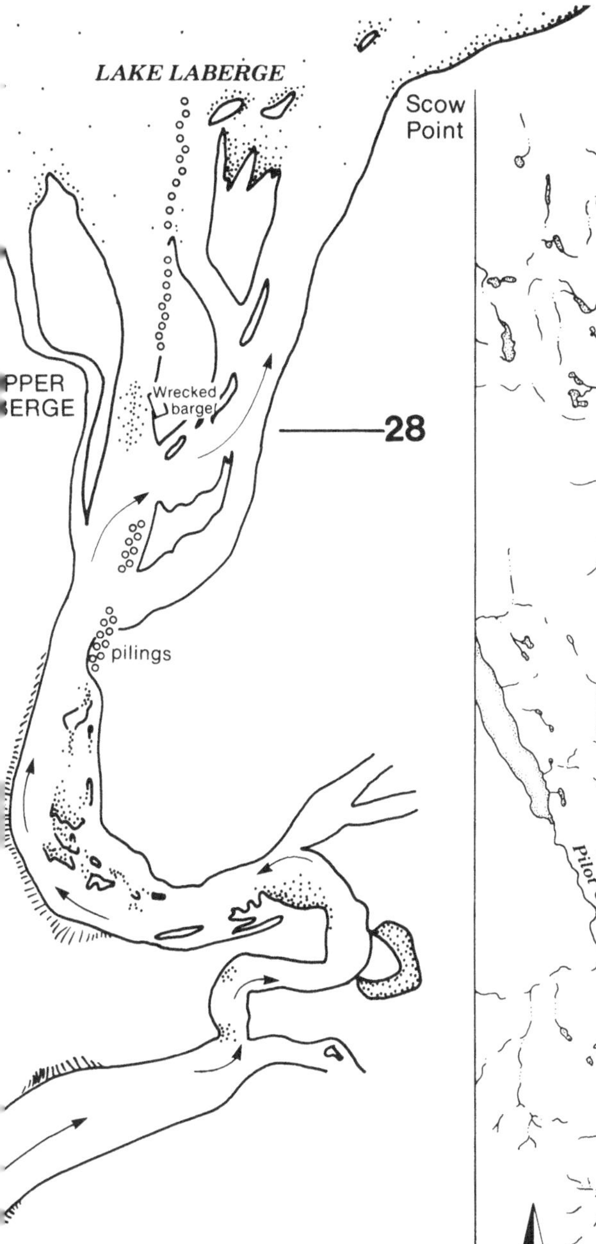
LAKE LABERGE
Scow Point
PPER
ERGE
Wrecked
barge
28
pilings
1 MILE

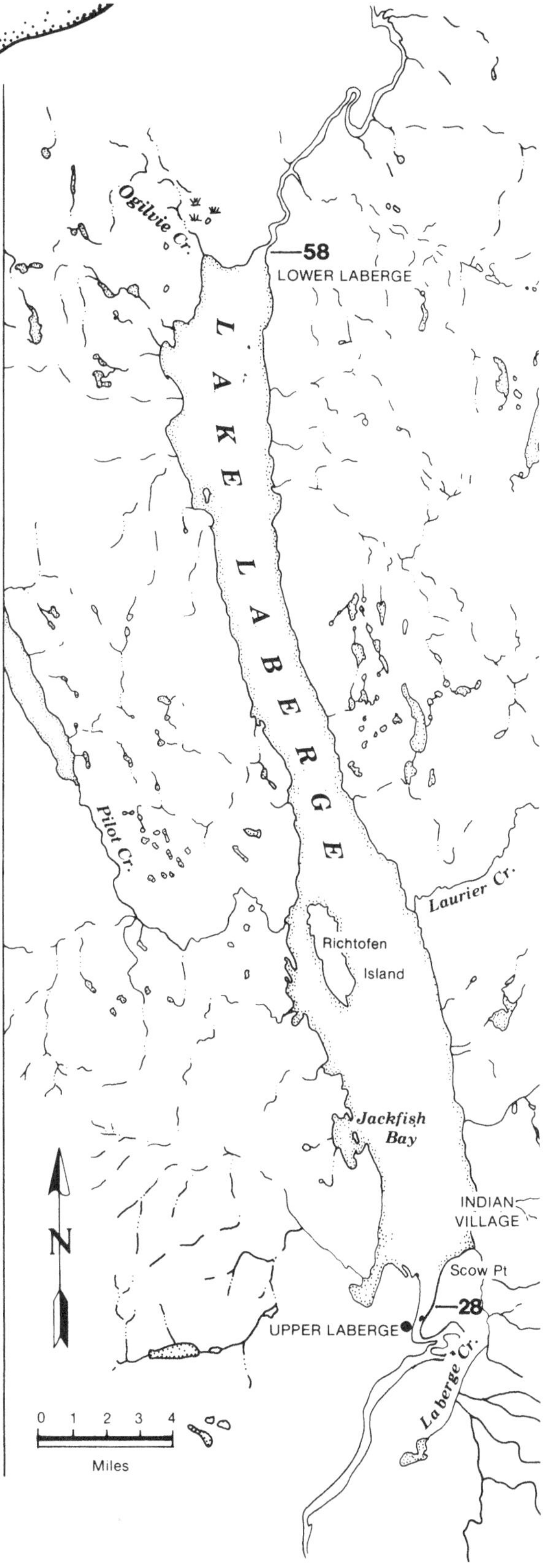
Ogilvie Cr.
58
LOWER LABERGE
LAKE LABERGE
Pilot Cr.
Laurier Cr.
Richtofen
Island
Jackfish
Bay
N
INDIAN
VILLAGE
Scow Pt
28
UPPER LABERGE
Laberge Cr.
0 1 2 3 4
Miles

island that assure privacy, shelter from weather and interesting beachcombing. The three-mile-long (five-km) island was named by Schwatka in honor of one Freiherr von Richtofen of Leipsic, a prominent figure of the day in geographical circles.

Readers of Robert Service will be more familiar with Lake Laberge than any other part of the Yukon, thanks to Service's ballad, "The Cremation of Sam McGee." The poem, like many of Service's ballads, had its conception in a very real situation. The real story (which one must assume has also been subject to embellishment over the years) tells us that a box-shaped steamboat named the *Olive May* was frozen in for the winter at the head of Lake Laberge. The Mounties found that an equally frozen-in prospector who lived in a cabin near the trapped *Olive May* was dying of scurvy. A doctor was found and sent to help, but arrived too late. Since it was impossible to bury the body until the following summer, the good doctor cremated the prospector in the *Olive May*'s firebox, then told an inconspicuous bank clerk named Robert Service about it. Thus is history—and poetry—made.

River travelers clean up after dinner during a still evening on Richtofen Island.

This old steamboat beacon did not need a light because steamboats ran only in the summer, when daylight lasted up to 24 hours.

An equally touching but infinitely less tragic story is connected with the lake's name. It was named for Mike Laberge, an explorer for the proposed Collins Telegraph line that was intended to go across Canada, Alaska and Siberia to Europe; a plan that sank into history when the first trans-Atlantic cable was successfully laid.

Laberge heard of a big, beautiful lake far upstream from his camp at Selkirk and spoke of it often and wistfully, hoping he could someday see it. He never set eyes on it, but he spoke of it so often that his companions referred to it as Laberge's lake.

Traces of the ice age can be seen on Richtofen Island where the glaciers left deep scars on the sloping granite boulders along the shore. The glaciers were more than a mile thick in this area, and the lake was one of those scooped out in a broad valley.

The surrounding countryside is similar to that around Whitehorse. The mountains are rounded, smooth and of limestone and granite. Timber and low brush grow to the lake's edge and wide expanses of sandy beaches and rocky headlands run from the water's edge to the vegetation line.

The island has numerous wild flowers during the short summer, including purple lupine, twinflower, ground cedar, northern bedstraw, fireweed, violets, creeping snowberry, Labrador tea, mosses, lichen, memophilias, wild onion, wild rose, aspen, balsam, willow and poplar.

mile 58
It is a beautiful place to camp away from the campground across from it, but the polluted water must be sterilized before use, and in case of storms, you may be isolated a day or two.

At the lake's northern end, the bottom gradually rises and can be seen clearly to a depth of about 6 meters. There are numerous sand and gravel bars near the end, which must be watched for carefully in power boats, and the beginning of the river is divided into three channels. The safest route is through either the left or the center channel between the rocks, but paddled craft can go through any of the three with no danger.

This shell of a cabin at Laberge Creek clearly shows the axe marks made when the logs were hewn into proper shape.

Lower Laberge

Immediately after entering the swift, clear river, watch for the remains of Lower Laberge on the east side, a group of cabins back in the timber, and the hull of the steamboat *Casca*. One of three boats named *Casca,* it was retired from steamer service to work as a barge before being beached to rot. This was the first *Casca* built. The second was built in Whitehorse and wrecked in 1936 in Rink Rapids. The third was built. also in Whitehorse, in 1937, then beached with the *Whitehorse* just downstream from the WP&YR depot in Whitehorse. Both burned in 1974, victims of arson.

With the burning of those two paddlewheelers, only three complete boats remain of the more than 200 that served on the river.

There is little of the Lower Laberge *Casca* today, only part of the deck and bow and some steel bolts. Back in the timber behind the sad boat are a few decaying cabins that mark the settlement of Lower Laberge. A few dog kennels, an ancient truck and the sagging cabins remain.

Thirtymile River

The river between Lower Laberge and Hootalinqua, still locally known as the Old Thirtymile River because it is 30 miles to Hootalinqua, is swift and clear as it winds through the canyons beneath wind-carved hoodoos in the cliffs above. It is a stretch of river to be savored, and one that should be drifted as silently as possible because it is so narrow that wildlife frequently is seen along the banks.

This stretch is the closest to a wilderness river you will find on the Yukon, the section least touched by man during the steamboat era. Old maps show only one woodcamp, and since it is so rugged along the banks most of the timber is still virgin. Along the remainder of the river the timber for the most part is second-growth. In many stretches, the spruce did not regenerate itself, and willows and aspen have taken over.

The steamboats had insatiable appetites for fuel and burned an estimated 300,000 cords of wood during the era. One could burn two cords of wood an hour, each stick four feet long, and it is little wonder that toward the end of the steamboat era on the river, the owners converted to oil. (WP&YR owned nearly every form of public transportation on the river, including a plane that flew between Whitehorse, Skagway and Juneau.) Woodcutter camps were stationed roughly every 30 miles (40 km) along the river. The contractors with WP&YR were paid $8 to $10 a cord; some paid others $5 a cord to cut it for them. The green wood was stacked to dry for a year before being used. Some woodcutters ran small traplines during the winter, but the sawing and cutting was a full-time if lonely occupation.

Some of the woodcutters were disappointed Klondike stampeders, other simply men who preferred living alone. Some went mad, no surprise to anyone who has spent a long period of time absolutely alone, as the woodcutters did in the winter.

While this section of the river is called the Old Thirtymile, it should be noted that the usual system of naming rivers by the mile ordinarily took another form. When the trio of traders—Jack McQuesten, Arthur Harper and Al Mayo—joined forces to support the prospectors until the big strike, they established a trading post called Fort Reliance in 1874, 6 miles (10 km) downstream from where Dawson City stands today and heartbreakingly close to the big strike that would come 22 years later.

Stampeders swamped on the Thirtymile. (Asahel Curtis)

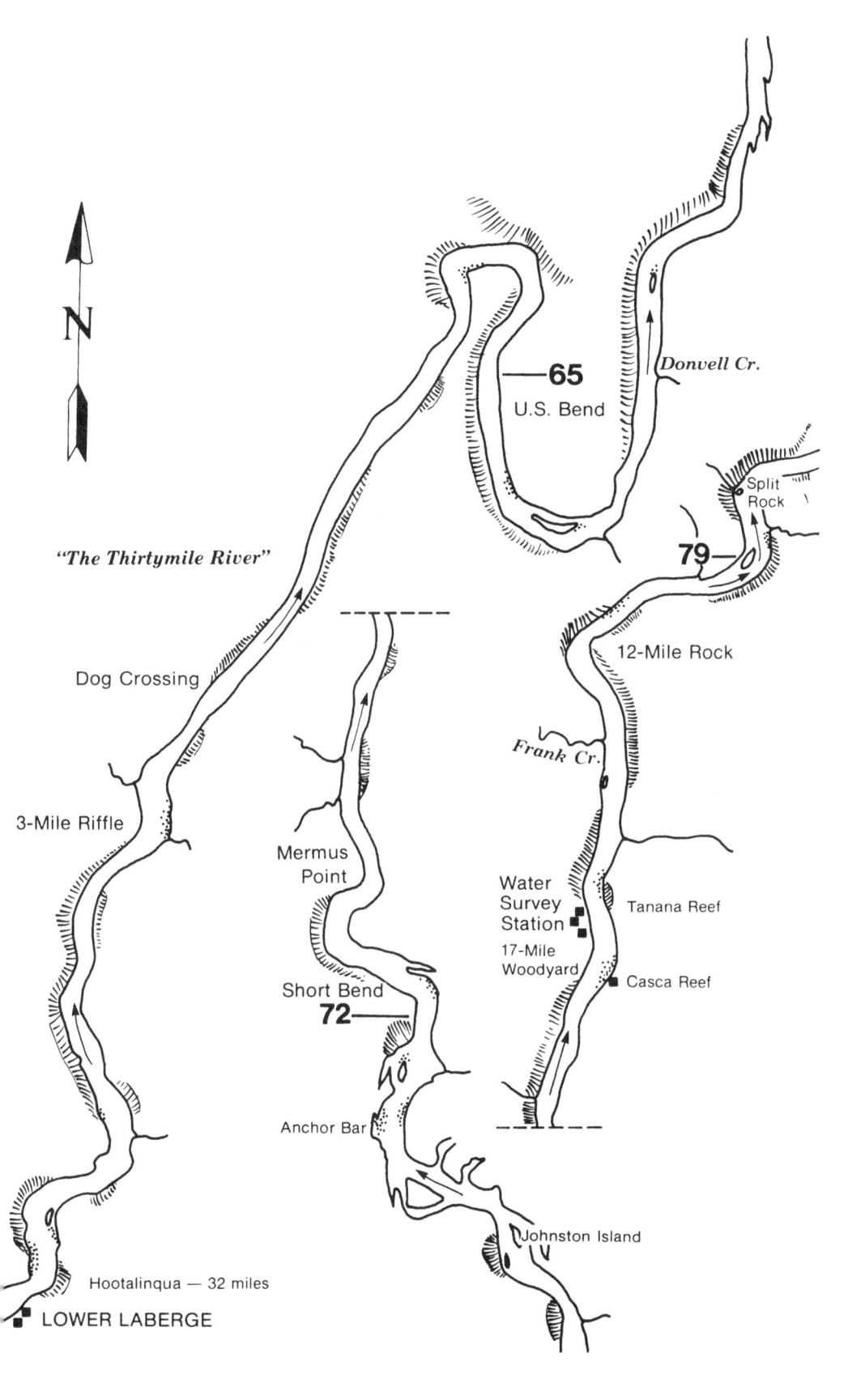

"The Thirtymile River"

- Donvell Cr.
- **65** U.S. Bend
- Split Rock
- **79**
- 12-Mile Rock
- Dog Crossing
- 3-Mile Riffle
- Frank Cr.
- Mermus Point
- Water Survey Station
- Tanana Reef
- 17-Mile Woodyard
- Short Bend **72**
- Casca Reef
- Anchor Bar
- Johnston Island
- Hootalinqua — 32 miles
- LOWER LABERGE

N

Only two or three cabins remain at Hootalinqua.

Since Fort Reliance was the first post that far upriver, streams often were named for their distance in miles from the fort, hence the Forty Mile, the Sixty Mile, etc. In most cases, those original names remain on all maps, sometimes as one word (Fortymile), sometimes two (Forty Mile).

An outstanding feature of the Thirtymile is U.S. Bend, about 7 miles (11 km) from Lower Laberge. The clear, clean water bores rapidly through a channel carved in a sharp S-curve with high bluffs on either side.

mile 65

Campsites are easily found along this portion of the river, and wildlife is frequently seen: moose, bears, eagles, ravens and swallows by the thousand. The area lends itself to short side hikes to the top of bluffs for views up and down the river.

Hootalinqua

mile 90

The Thirtymile ends at Hootalinqua, where the broad Teslin enters. A wide clearing and excellent campsite are on the left (west) bank overlooking the two rivers and a slough. Arctic grayling and pike can be easily caught for dinner. Hootalinqua

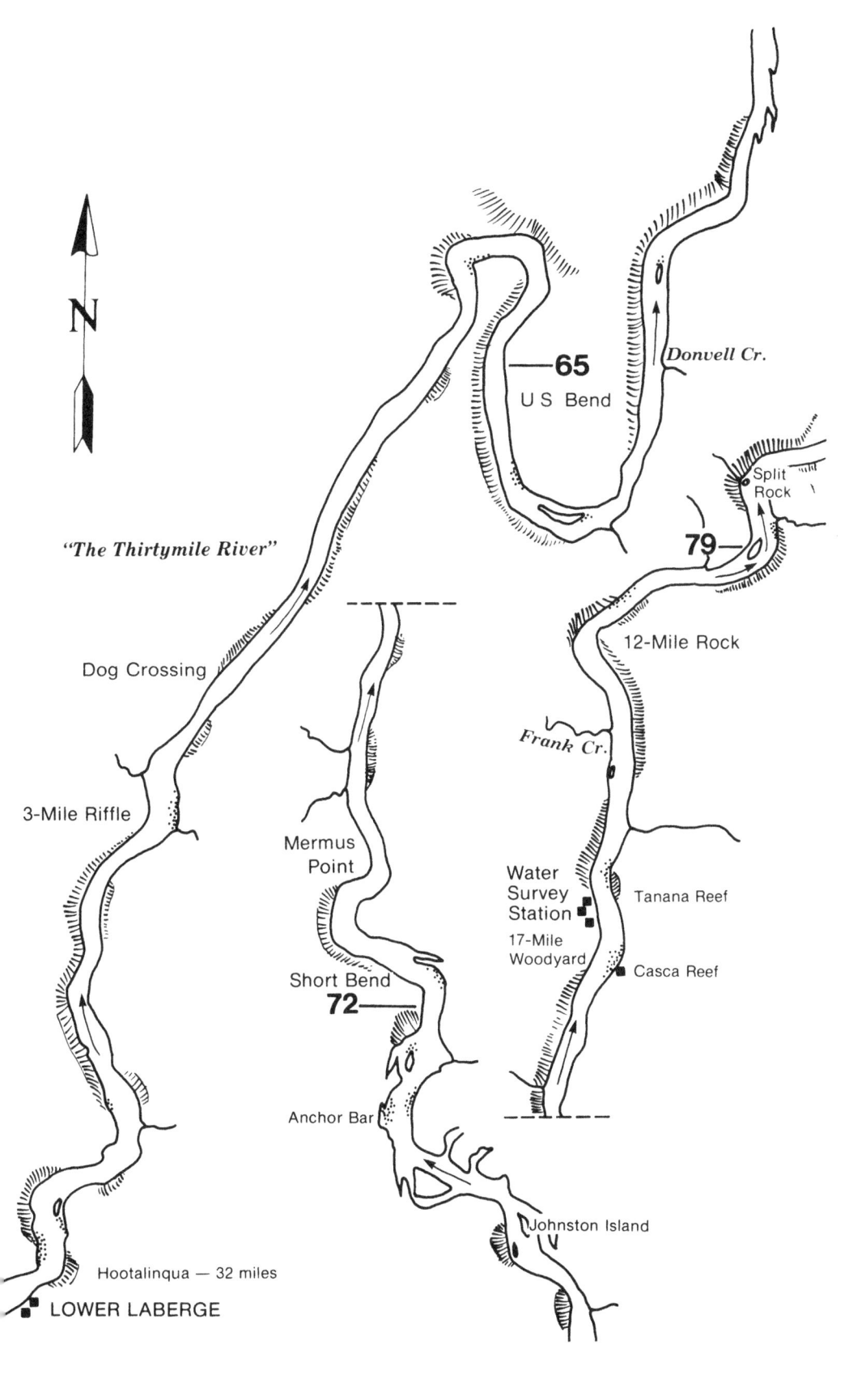

"The Thirtymile River"

65 U S Bend

Donvell Cr.

Split Rock

79

12-Mile Rock

Frank Cr.

Dog Crossing

3-Mile Riffle

Mermus Point

Water Survey Station

Tanana Reef

17-Mile Woodyard

Casca Reef

Short Bend

72

Anchor Bar

Johnston Island

Hootalinqua — 32 miles

LOWER LABERGE

N

was an RCMP post; two of the buildings still standing offer some protection from the weather.

The river gains both momentum and silt with the Teslin's entrance, and it becomes browner as it flows north.

Immediately downstream from Hootalinqua is an island you should visit, called Shipyard Island on some maps but named Hootalinqua Island by a sign on the bank. In the middle of the island is an old, decaying steamboat named the *Evelyn* which was pulled up on the ways for repair and left there forever. WP/YR had bought it from its bankrupt owners but never used it. The *Evelyn* was built in 1908 in Seattle for the Upper Tanana Trading Co. It was wrecked in the Tanana and taken down to the boat yard at St. Michael, where a new hull was built. Then it was sold to the North American Transportation & Trading Co. and renamed the *Norcom*. Somewhere along the line its original name was restored, and it is so named by a sign on its hull today.

A few miles farther downstream is the wreck of the steamer *Klondike,* the first one under that name, which was wrecked in the Thirtymile River in 1936 and has drifted to her present location. Its skeleton sticks up above the water during late summer but often is covered during high-water periods.

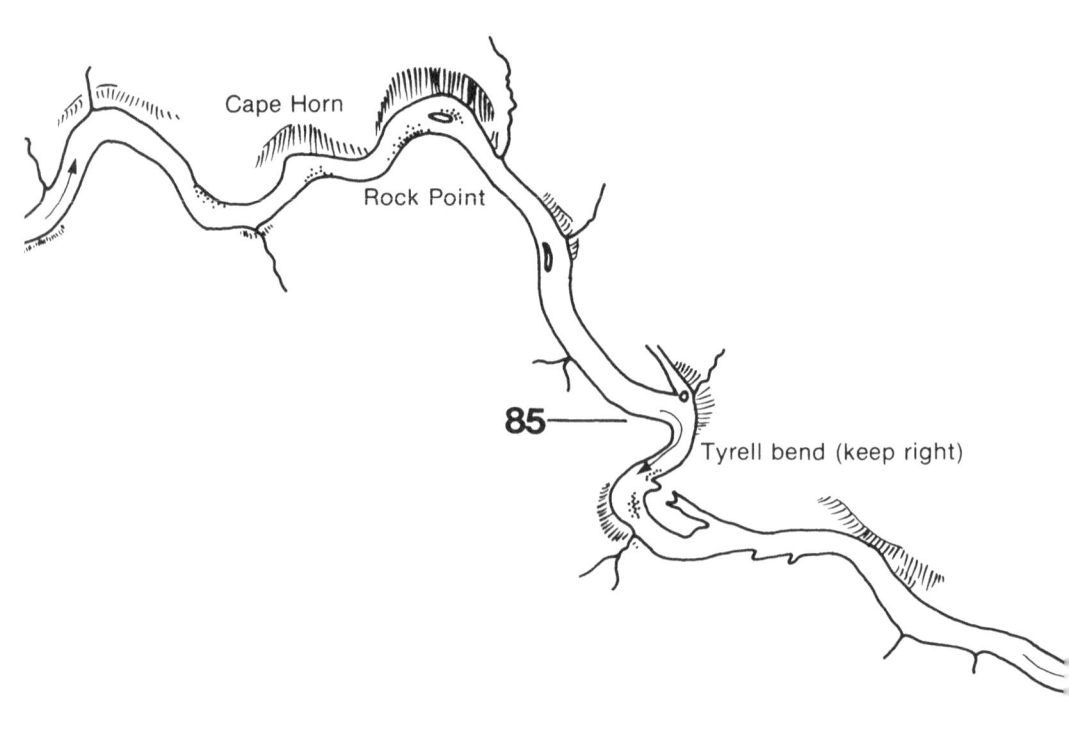

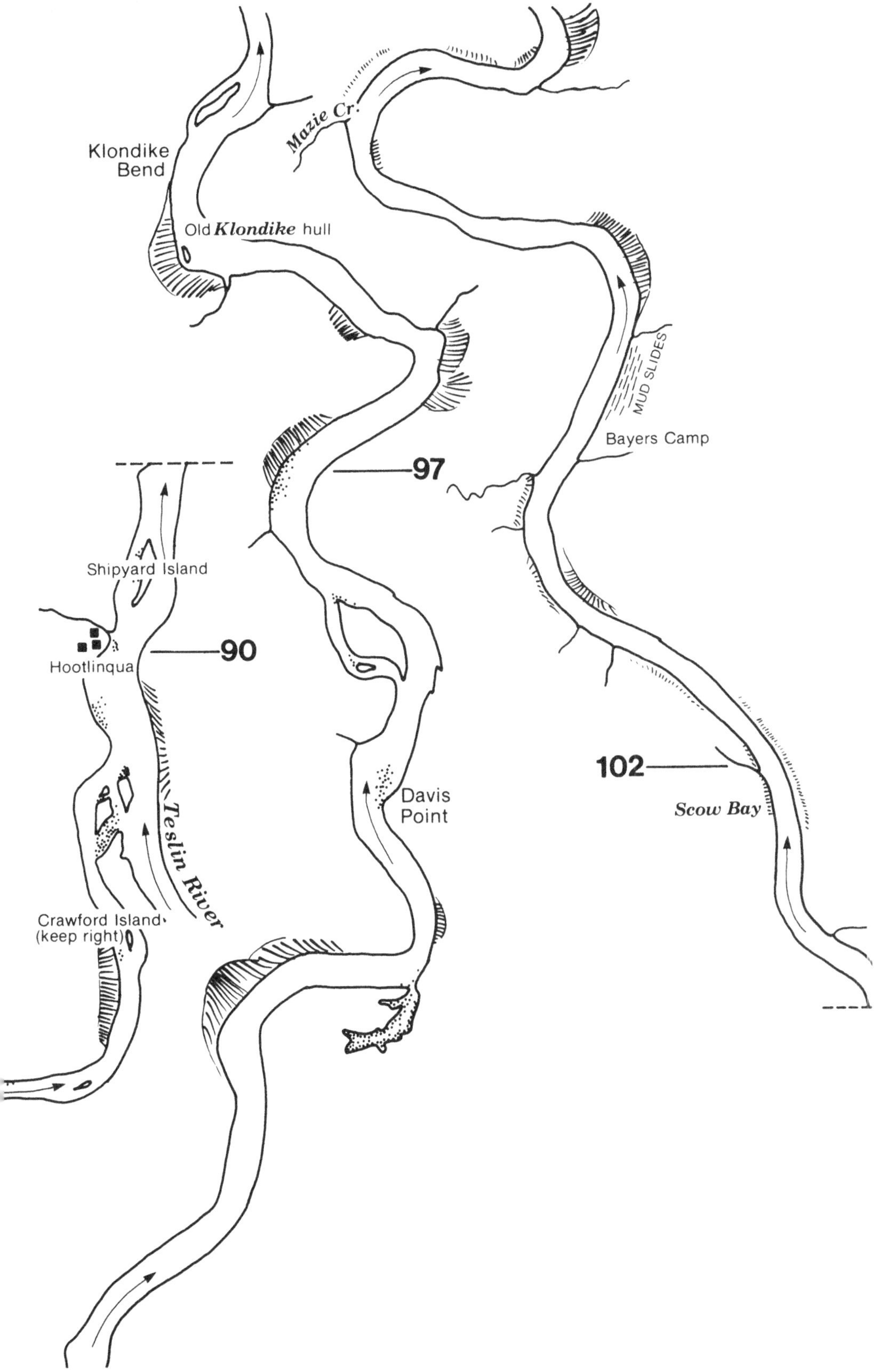

Klondike Bend
Mazie Cr.
Old Klondike hull
MUD SLIDES
Bayers Camp
97
Shipyard Island
90
Hootlinqua
102
Scow Bay
Davis Point
Teslin River
Crawford Island (keep right)

Hootalinqua to Carmacks

After leaving Hootalinqua, the river valley opens up considerably, and the cutbanks on one side and willow-covered lowlands on the other become common. The occasional whirlpools present no danger but are merely brisk diversions from the normally swift river; there are also occasional upwellings that result from the flow of water over rocks on the bottom.

The village of Big Salmon is on the east side of the river, 35 miles (56 km) downstream from Hootalinqua where a river of the same name enters. It was a trading post and Indian village when traffic was on the water, and buildings are still standing on both sides of the river. The abandoned buildings offer protection, and often boaters pitch their tents outside for sleeping and use one of the buildings of this and other villages for cooking. By setting fire to a mosquito coil (and being absolutely certain it is placed on a piece of metal so it won't set fire to the building itself), you can clear mosquitos quite rapidly from a room. **Big Salmon mile 125**

All villages along the river are protected by the territorial government: nobody should have to be discouraged from defacing or destroying any of the structures. Extreme care should always be taken to avoid fires. Furniture and planks should not be ripped off anywhere and used for firewood. There always are adequate supplies of downed timber and branches for open campfires, but sometimes you will have to walk a few feet to get them.

When approaching one of these villages that almost always are at the mouth of a stream, whether paddling or under power, head into the eddy that is usually found just downriver from where the stream enters the river. It can be tricky and hard work for a paddler.

Unless you prefer company on the river, camp along the bank or on one of the many islands that appear all along the river. There is always an abundance of driftwood on the islands for fires, and the wind on the open, exposed sandbars will keep mosquitos away from your stew. Some residents say mosquitos in your stew or your coffee add protein to your diet. Perhaps so, but they don't say anything about their having a jolly effect on your disposition.

mile 160 It is 35 miles (56 km) from Big Salmon to Little Salmon, and you should plan stops at each of the old towns and woodcutters' camps for the sake of curiosity if nothing else.

About 10 miles (16 km) downstream from Big Salmon is an old dredge on the right (east) bank that was abandoned years ago. It was hauled up and down the river by its owners to dredge for gold on the feeder streams, not, as some assume, to dredge the river to keep the channels open. There is no adequate camping here, and the thick, damp underbrush is laden with mosquitos.

A nice side hike can be taken from the site of Lakeview up the small stream on an old trail. The stream has an abundance of grayling and pike which can be caught in the stream or where it enters the river. From Teslin down, the only places where fishing can be worth the effort is where the streams enter the silt-laden river, or in the larger streams.

Other side hikes can be taken up to the top of the bald knobs on either side of the river, some of which are up to 650 meters high.

The coal mine near Carmacks on Tantalus Butte, below Hootalinqua.

Walsh Creek

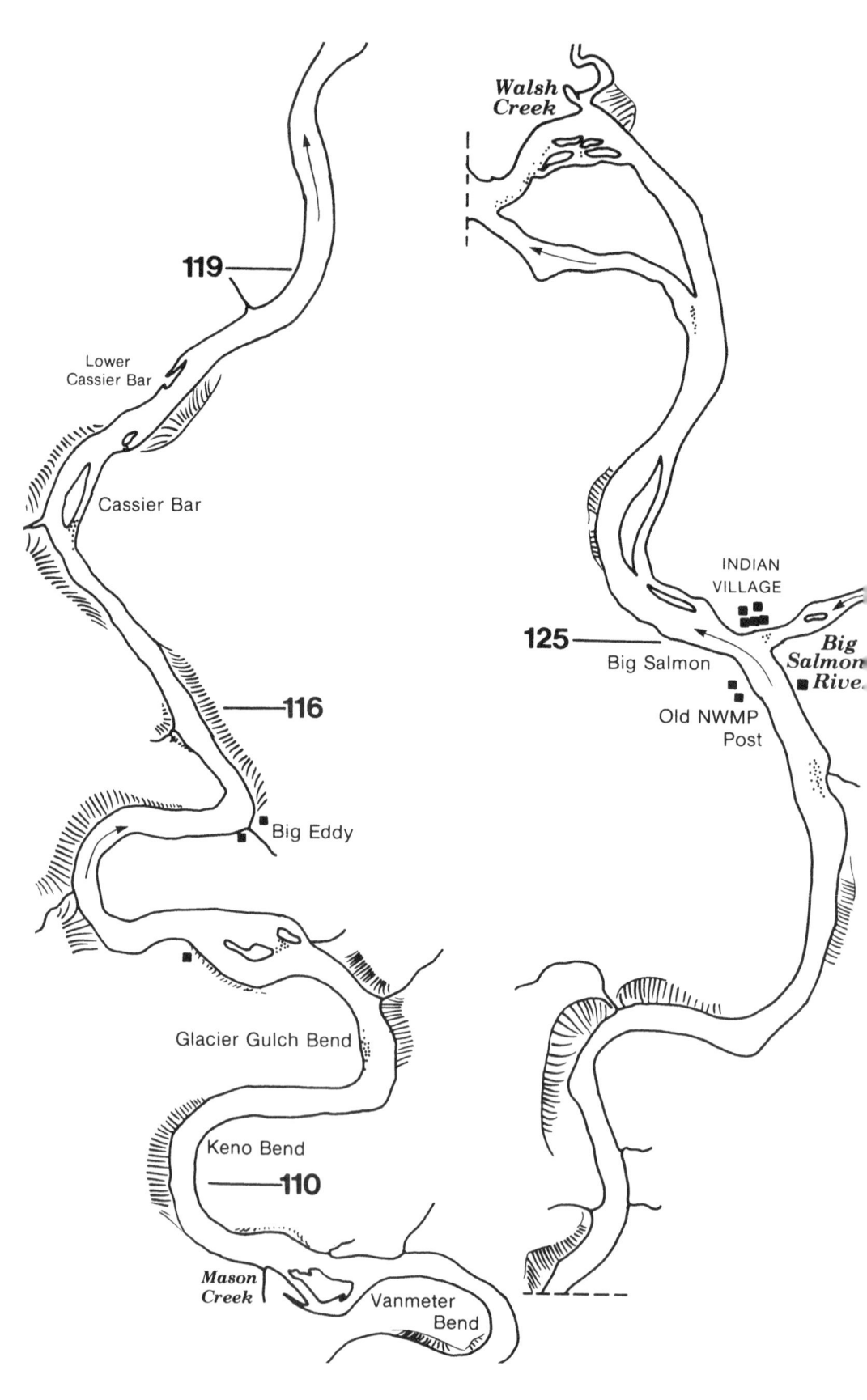

119

Lower Cassier Bar

Cassier Bar

125 Big Salmon

INDIAN VILLAGE

Big Salmon River

116

Old NWMP Post

Big Eddy

Glacier Gulch Bend

Keno Bend

110

Mason Creek

Vanmeter Bend

Frickson's Wood Camp

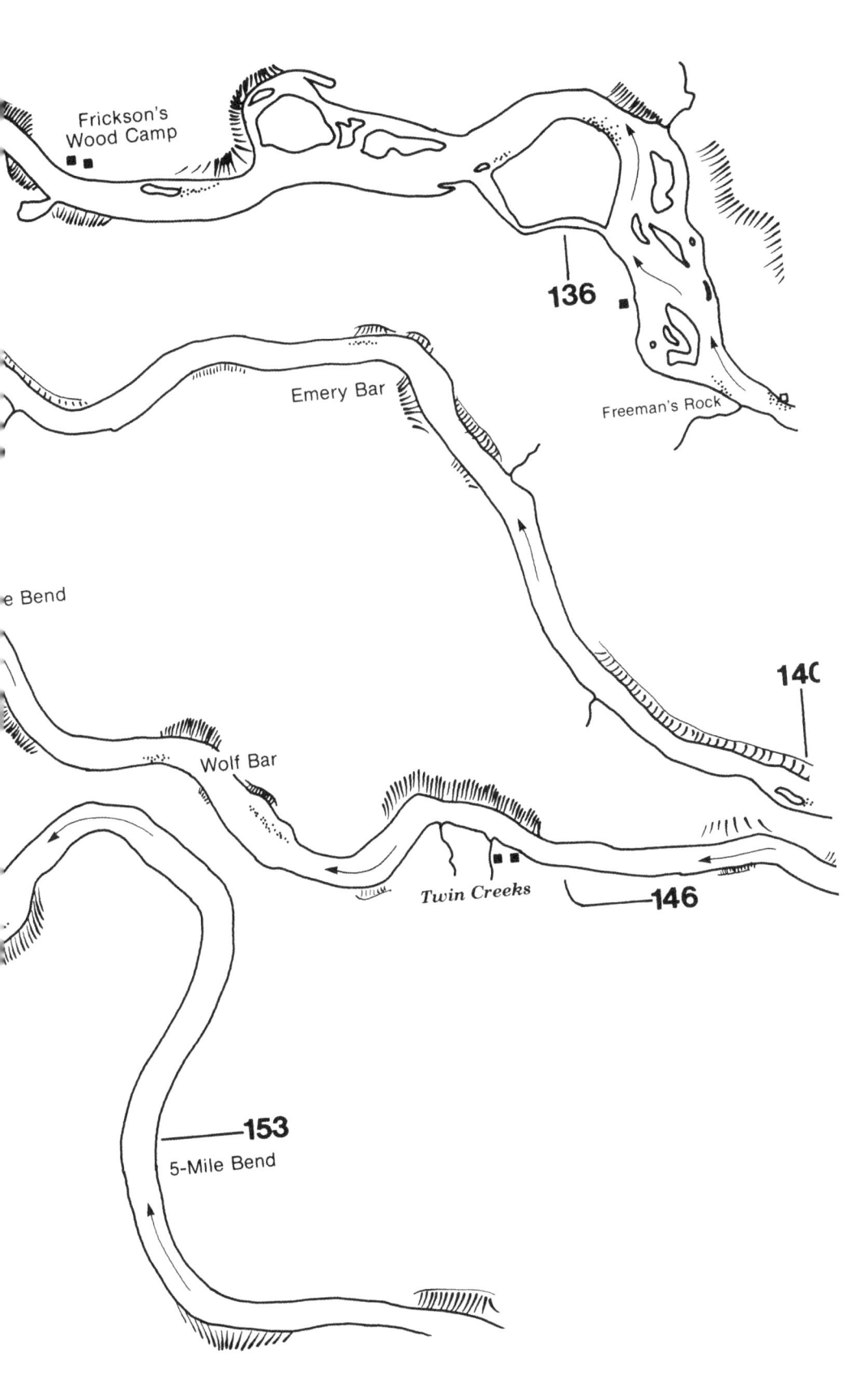

136

Emery Bar

Freeman's Rock

e Bend

140

Wolf Bar

Twin Creeks **146**

153
5-Mile Bend

Dutch Bluff

Nordling's Wash

4th of July Bend

—132

Little Salmon

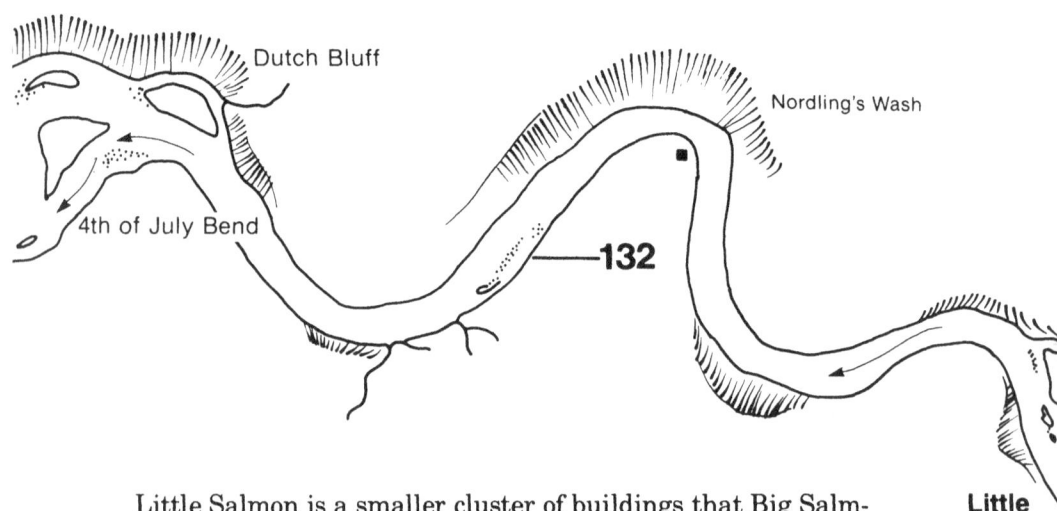

Little Salmon is a smaller cluster of buildings that Big Salmon, but it has an Indian cemetery of special interest. Here are a group of the small wooden "spirit houses" built over graves; through the windows one can see the clothing and household goods that belonged to the person buried there. One cabin, or spirit house, has several toys inside which would indicate a child was buried there.

Below Little Salmon, the river has lost something of its feeling of isolation because the Whitehorse-to-Dawson City highway can be seen on the eastern slopes of the hills from many stretches of the river.

The presence of the highway and power lines immediately puts you back into the feeling that civilization is nearby. Yet there are interesting stretches of river on the way to Carmacks.

The number of islands increases considerably and during the high-water periods they will remind you of steamboats because they have what amounts to bow waves as the rushing river hits their prows and splashes upward on the rocks and driftwood that inevitably gather there.

173

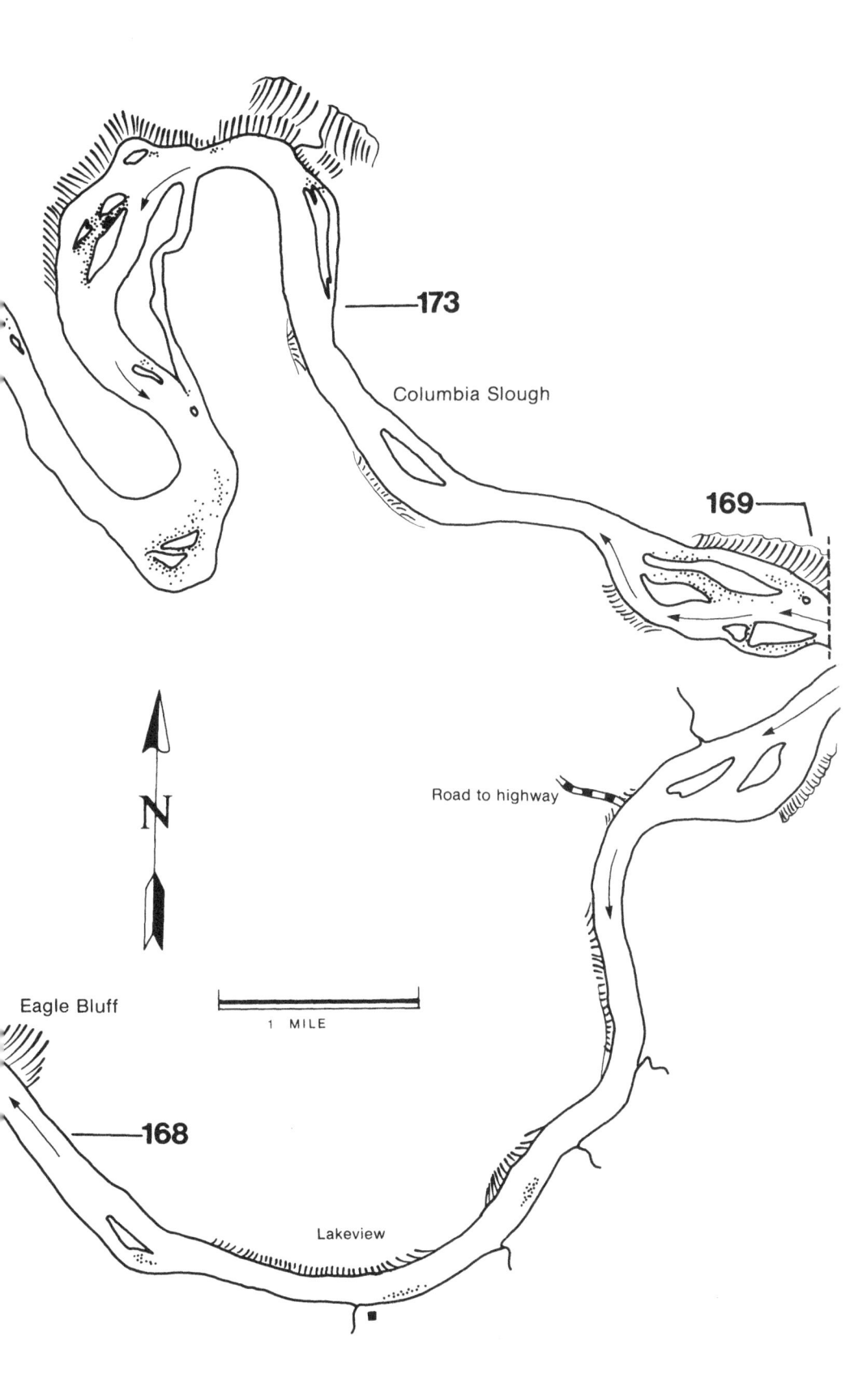

Columbia Slough

169

Road to highway

N

1 MILE

Eagle Bluff

168

Lakeview

LITTLE SALMON VILLAGE — Little Salmon River

Carmacks-42 Miles — **160**

Tiny spirit houses at ghost town of Little Salmon.

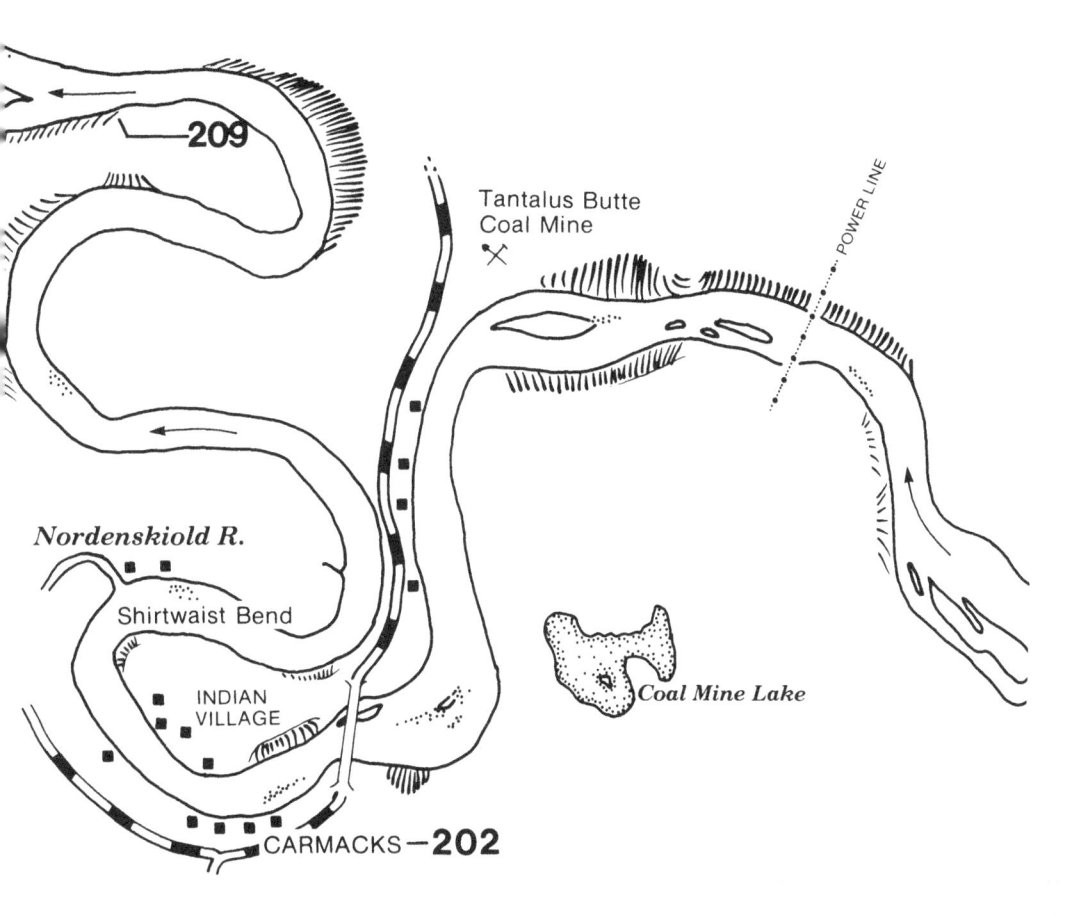

Carmacks

As you approach Carmacks, the highway remains in sight most of the time, and the Tantalus Butte coal mine comes into view on the east side. The butte was named by Schwatka during his journey downstream. He wrote that "a conspicuous bald butte could be seen directly in front of our raft no less than seven times, on as many different stretches of the river. I called it Tantalus Butte and was glad to see it disappear from sight."

In Greek mythology Tantalus was the king of Phrygia, son of Zeus and the nymph Pluto. He served the flesh of his son, Pelops, to the gods and was condemned to stand in water that receded when he tried to drink and beneath branches of fruit that always eluded his grasp.

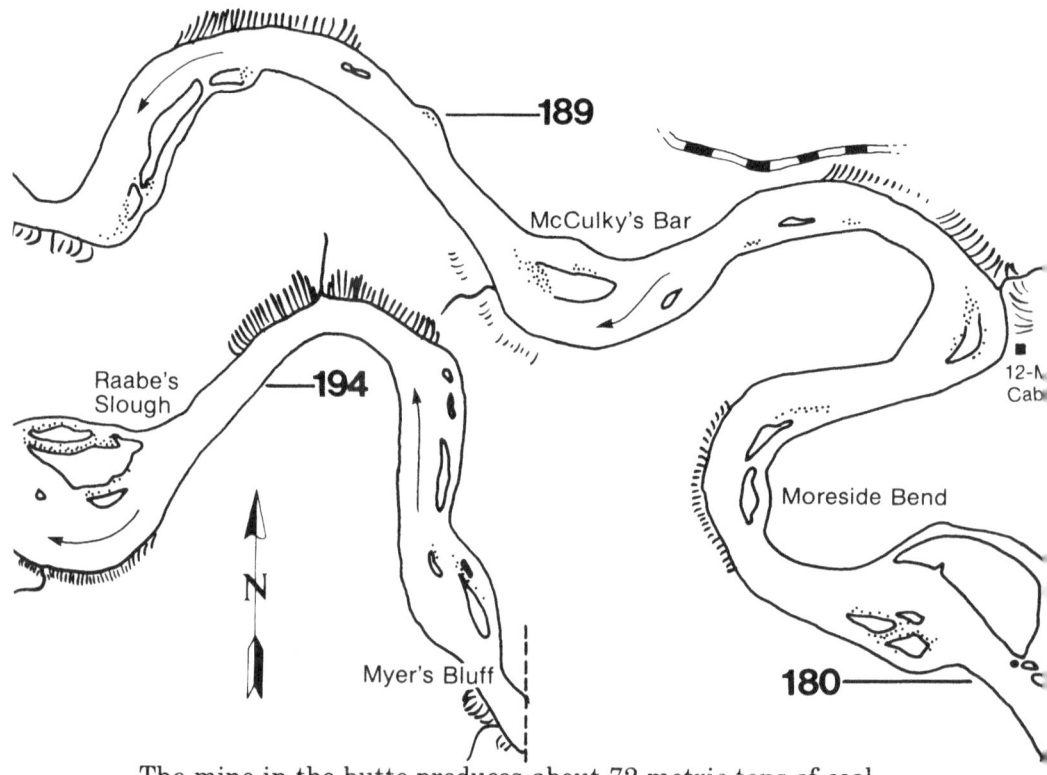

The mine in the butte produces about 72 metric tons of coal daily for the dryer plant at the Anvil Mine near Faro, the largest mine in the Yukon which produces silver, lead and zinc. It has been in operation off and on since about 1900. The coal was used for heating in Dawson City and Whitehorse before the Anvil Mine Corporation bought the mine in the mid-1960s. Today, about a dozen miners work there, mostly Indians living in the Carmacks area.

The highway bridge at Carmacks ended the steamboat era. **mile 202** When it was built, there were no allowances made for the high-hatted steamboats, and when the *Keno* went on its final journey downstream to Dawson City to become a museum, part of its top deck had to be removed and its stacks hinged to clear the bridge.

Carmacks has about 200 residents and is the last town you will see until Dawson City about 260 miles (418 km) away. Here you will have to reprovision, top off the fuel tanks and replace any items you might have dropped in the drink (everybody on the river loses something, it seems: gloves, sunglasses, knife, etc.). It also is your last chance for a restaurant meal and a shower. A roadhouse offers showers at a nominal cost, but be forewarned: the mosquitos love nothing better than fresh, clean meat. As soon as you finish your shower, you'll have to make yourself rank again with repellent or else live with the itchy bumps.

Unfortunately, the landings at Carmacks are not convenient to the stores and service stations. From the public dock beneath the bridge, it is a half-mile walk to town for supplies. Use of the government dock is frowned upon. The alternative is to tie up to the bank as close to the town as possible, then form a fire brigade and pass the supplies down to the boats.

If you have a large load of purchases to make, and especially if you have to refill a drum of fuel, it is best to find someone to hire transportation to the river. All stores and service stations naturally are on the highway and it is quite a walk with arms laden with goods. You can solve the problem by carrying a backpack. (Leave someone to watch the canoes; theft and vandalism can be expected along the highways.)

An undercut bank sloughs into the river during a high-water period.

Carmacks to Fort Selkirk

Just after leaving Carmacks you will think you're suffering from some rare eye disease or that someone is running the movie backwards. On the way into Carmacks you will see a church with a prominent cross in a grove of trees. Leaving town, you'll see the same church in the same grove of trees again.

Be not dismayed. You're going around Shirtwaist Bend, one of the sharpest bends in the river, where the river nearly doubles back on itself. It is also a place to lose your sense of direction. However, the river soon straightens out and heads north as it is supposed to.

The water flows rapidly below Carmacks and down to the rapids, and is characterized by boils, surges, an occasional flat pool and riffles. It is a beautiful stretch of river. The high canyon walls on either side occasionally give way to sand and gravel bluffs directly above the river, with a second and higher set of bluffs behind those.

Five Finger Rapids are about 20 miles (32 km) downstream from Carmacks. Just before you reach them, you will begin seeing wind-carved hoodoos with swallows nesting in them in the hillside directly above the river.

Five Finger Rapids

Campsites are more difficult to find above the rapids than in other stretches of the river because of the high bluffs. An old settlement called Kellyville on the west side of the river a few miles above the rapids is used by Indians as a summer fish camp and should not be counted on for a campsite. If you prefer camping above the rapids and saving them for another day, watch for an exposed gravel bar or a likely knoll back in the timber.

218

✕ Coal Mine

Tatchun Cr.

224

Five Finger Rapids
(keep right)

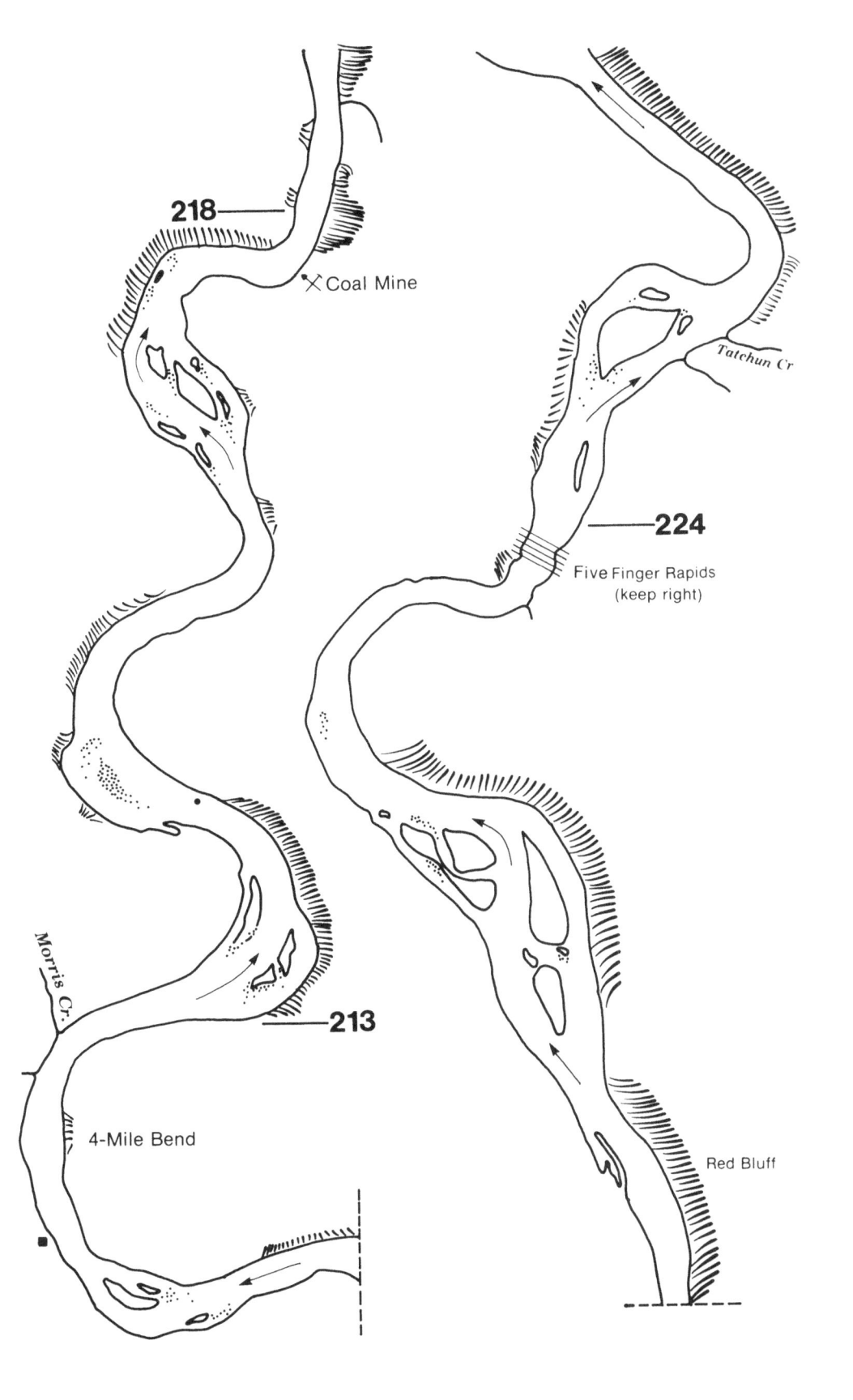

Morris Cr.

213

4-Mile Bend

Red Bluff

A motorist's-eye view of Five Finger Rapids, shown from the turnout on the highway between Whitehorse and Dawson City.

The rapids are not much by Colorado River standards: a few bumps, some whitewater and you're out. But they should not become a toy, either, because they can tip a canoe or kayak easily and the combination of cold water and the prospect of losing one's provisions should not be overlooked.

Five Finger Rapids get their name from the four "flower pot" islands in the river and the five channels of water that go around them. The islands are unique on the river; that type does not appear elsewhere. The extreme right (east) channel is the safest and widest. Steamboats used this channel. The transportation companies anchored a heavy cable in a shack just above the rapids (few see it because they're watching the water, not the bank); the steamboat crewmen hooked the cable to a winch on the bow and winched themselves up through the swift water.

There is a good chance you will have an audience as you navigate Five Fingers because the highway runs high up on the cliff above, and a turnout has been built there for a panoramic view of the rapids and river.

mile 224

The rapids consist of waves a half meter high with strong back eddies on either side caused by the water rushing around the islands. A slight crosscurrent is caused by the water dashing against the right-hand cliff and being forced out across the main channel. Enter the rapids in the center to avoid both the crosscurrent and the back eddies below the rapids.

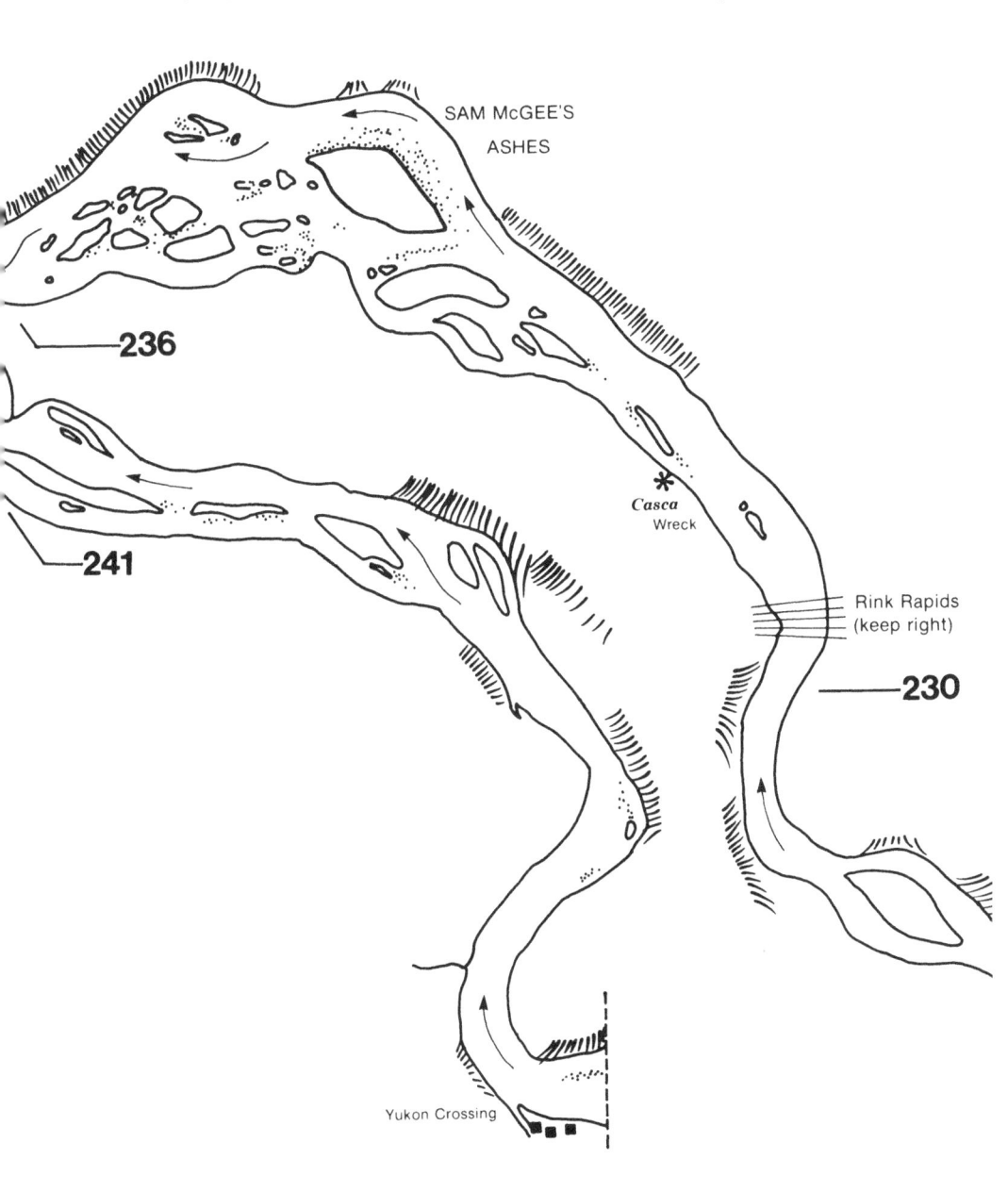

Tatchun Creek

A short distance below the rapids is a government campground on the short Tatchun Creek. A road from the creek mouth leads back to the campground and across the highway to Tatchun Lake. During July and August many salmon are caught in the river at the creek mouth.

Rink Rapids

Rink Rapids is 6 miles (10 km) downstream. Again, take the right side. By bearing right, the rapids themselves can be missed entirely and only choppy water will be encountered. During the steamboat era, Rink Rapids were much rougher than they are now, a situation that was altered by putting some dynamite in the rapids and blasting out some of the rocks. The rapids are not especially dangerous and many boaters, seeking one last thrill before the flat water below, run through the middle. However, as with any set of rapids, you should pull over to shore above and scout them; don't commit yourself to a course without knowing what lies ahead.

After Rink Rapids, the river flattens out considerably and the current slows to about half speed, three knots. The valley floor becomes wider and the banks lower. More islands appear, and you have only shallow water or dead-end sloughs to watch for.

Sam McGee's Ashes

Just below Rink Rapids is a deep deposit of volcanic ash in the bank that has been named "Sam McGee's Ashes," although old Sam, as noted earlier, was cremated far upstream at Lake Laberge.

Such ash deposits are seen elsewhere along the bank, in layers up to a foot deep. The deposits came from eruptions far to the west in the St. Elias Range, one of which covered all the area now occupied by Whitehorse. So poor is the soil in Whitehorse and other places in the Yukon that topsoil is imported for lawns and gardens.

By watching the river bank, you will see how shallow the topsoil is all along the river, which explains in part why the timber does not reach marketable size in the Yukon's interior. Other factors include the extremely cold winters and the semiarid climate that retards decomposition. The Yukon has not had sufficient time from the last ice age to build up a deep topsoil above the permafrost which is evident in varying depths throughout most of the Yukon.

Yukon Crossing

Four miles (six km) below "Sam McGee's Ashes" is the ghost town of Yukon Crossing, which gives an excellent example of pioneer architecture in the two-story log cabin roadhouse. The roadhouse served both the river traffic in the summer and the winter-road traffic during the other nine months of the year.

The government cleared and maintained a road of sorts that ran from Whitehorse to Dawson City along a route similar to the highway right-of-way today. It crossed the river at Yukon Crossing, followed it down to the Pelly River, then swung inland in a more or less straight line to Dawson City.

Dogs, then horses and finally small tracked vehicles were used to pull sleds and wagons during the winter. Passengers were expected to be warmly dressed, hardy and uncomplaining.

Minto mile 258

Below Yukon Crossing the river widens and flattens even more as it enters Minto Flats. Islands become more frequent and it is often difficult to tell which is an island and which is the mainland. These characteristics continue well below the town of Minto, then the river narrows again and picks up speed when the Pelly joins it.

There isn't much at Minto of interest to the wilderness buff. There are some pit toilets near the river bank for those who consider that sort of thing a luxury, and there are a few picnic tables and fire pits scattered around the open field that leads back to the abandoned buildings.

Minto was an Indian village, and the houses and caches are still used during the salmon runs by descendants of the earlier residents. The town has the distinction of having had a series of unsolved murders in the early 1950s.

Minto has an emergency airstrip. Helicopters as well as fixed-wing planes use it as a refueling station, as evidenced by stacks of orange barrels around the river bank. The highway is a short distance up a dirt road; this is your last contact with the highway until Dawson City.

The remaining 24 miles (39 km) to Fort Selkirk are more of the same—a wide river with many islands and an occasional glimpse of the old winter road going across a hillside on the east bank of the river. After Minto, all traces of the highway disappear until Dawson City.

The landscape beside the river rises slowly from Minto to the confluence of the Pelly at Fort Selkirk. The high banks gradu-

Minto

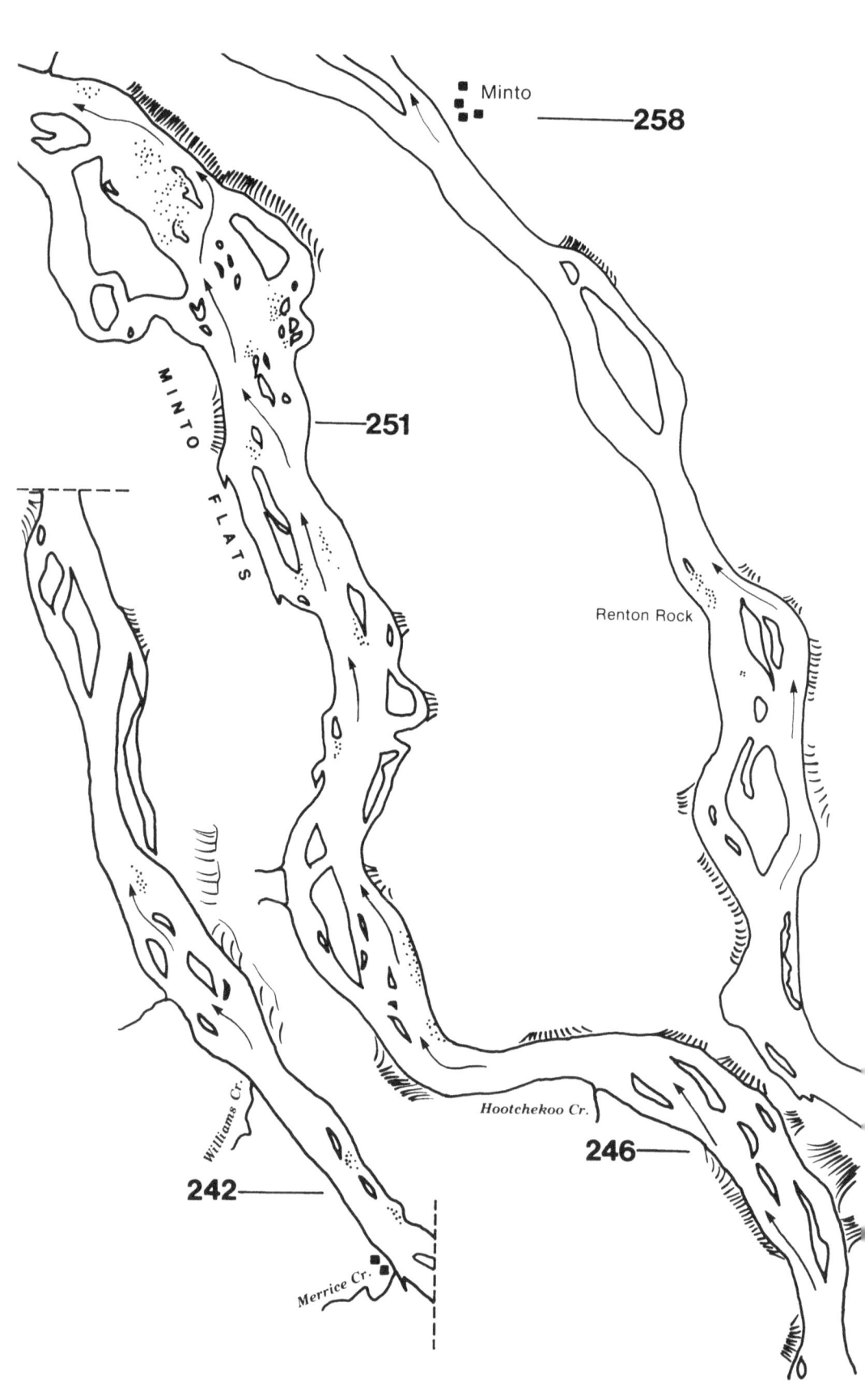

258

MINTO FLATS

251

Renton Rock

Williams Cr.

Hootchekoo Cr.

246

242

Merrice Cr.

Arrival at Fort Selkirk

ally grow higher; the river is broad and island-dotted.

One of the visual treats of the river trip is to approach Fort Selkirk late at night when the sun lies low over the water. Its slanting light hits the windows of the town like lamps burning in the windows of a small coastal town. No matter the time of day one arrives, there is something welcoming about the town. Many boaters spend an extra day there, getting their land legs back again, catching up on laundry and strolling around the clearing on the high bank above the river. The view from there extends back up the Yukon and across to the Pelly and the high, basalt cliff that defines the river on the other side.

The best landing site is toward the north end of the town at a ramp carved into the high bank during the steamboat era. Watch for the schoolhouse, the closest building to the bank, and you will see the ramp directly below it. The river is swift along the bank and requires some exertion for canoeists or kayakers to stop or slow enough to leap out and haul the craft in. The river runs against the bank and keeps it scoured out and deep, so don't jump overboard more than a meter from the bank.

Selkirk (many drop the Fort from its title) is the best preserved old town along the river, and the largest. It is in good shape because Danny Roberts and his wife and daughter live there and he serves as watchman and caretaker. You will meet Danny shortly after arrival because he is required to have every visitor sign a register, and he will point out the best sources of firewood and the buildings that offer the most protection from weather. Just outside the schoolhouse is a big firepit for use by visitors.

Visitors are welcome to use any of the buildings as sleeping quarters, with the obvious understanding that the buildings are not to be littered and anything found inside them stays inside them.

History—A Trading Post and Government Station

Fort Selkirk was founded as a trading post by Robert Campbell of the Hudson's Bay Co. in 1848. After Campbell and his companions built Fort Selkirk and established trade with the local Indians, life fell into its normal pattern and the Indians

272

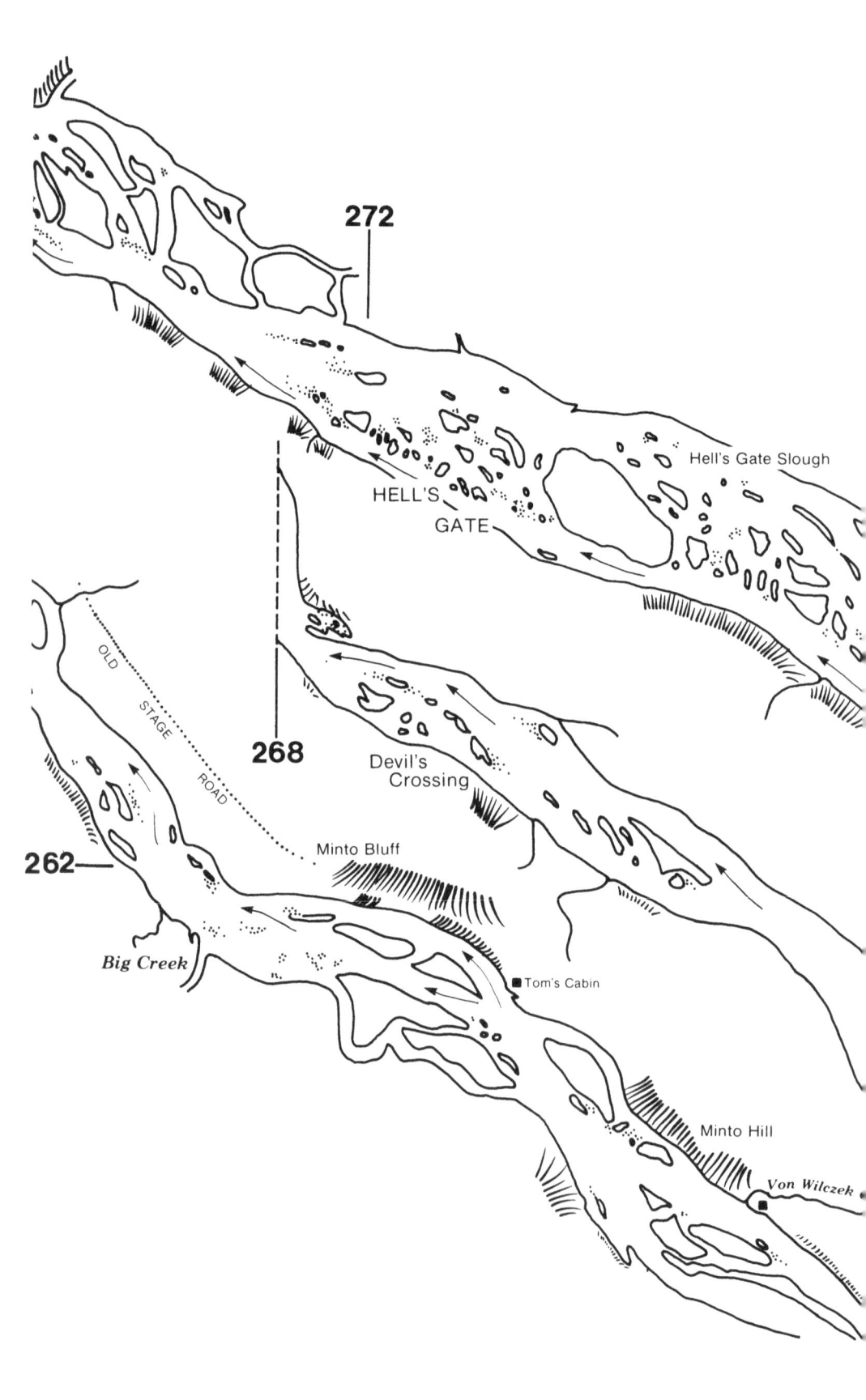

Hell's Gate Slough

HELL'S
GATE

OLD STAGE ROAD

268

Devil's Crossing

Minto Bluff

262

Big Creek

Tom's Cabin

Minto Hill

Von Wilczek

seemed content. They had no difficulty in obtaining ample food for the winters, with fish easily netted in the backwaters of a slough near the post, and moose and caribou in abundant supply back in the forest.

But they had made an enemy in the case of the Chilkat Indians, far to the south on Lynn Canal in what is now Alaska. The Chilkats had exercised a monopoly over the Interior Indians. Some had visited the post during the four years it had existed and had never shown particularly good manners while there. Their resentment was a matter of record and it not only made Campbell and his men nervous, it frightened the local Indians.

On the morning of August 20, 1852, Campbell and three men were cutting the tall native grass that grows abundantly there for the post's milk cow. They saw five rafts bearing down on the post with 27 Chilkats aboard.

They came ashore armed with guns. Three of Campbell's employees headed for the timber behind the post, leaving Campbell and two others to face the Chilkats. He tried diplomacy, which was ineffective. But the Chilkats did not attack that day. Instead, they permitted Campbell and his crew to go to bed that night while they ("the infernal devils") prowled the post all night trying to break into the buildings through locked doors and barred windows.

An ash deposit from a volcanic eruption centuries ago has been nicknamed Sam McGee's Ashes.

281

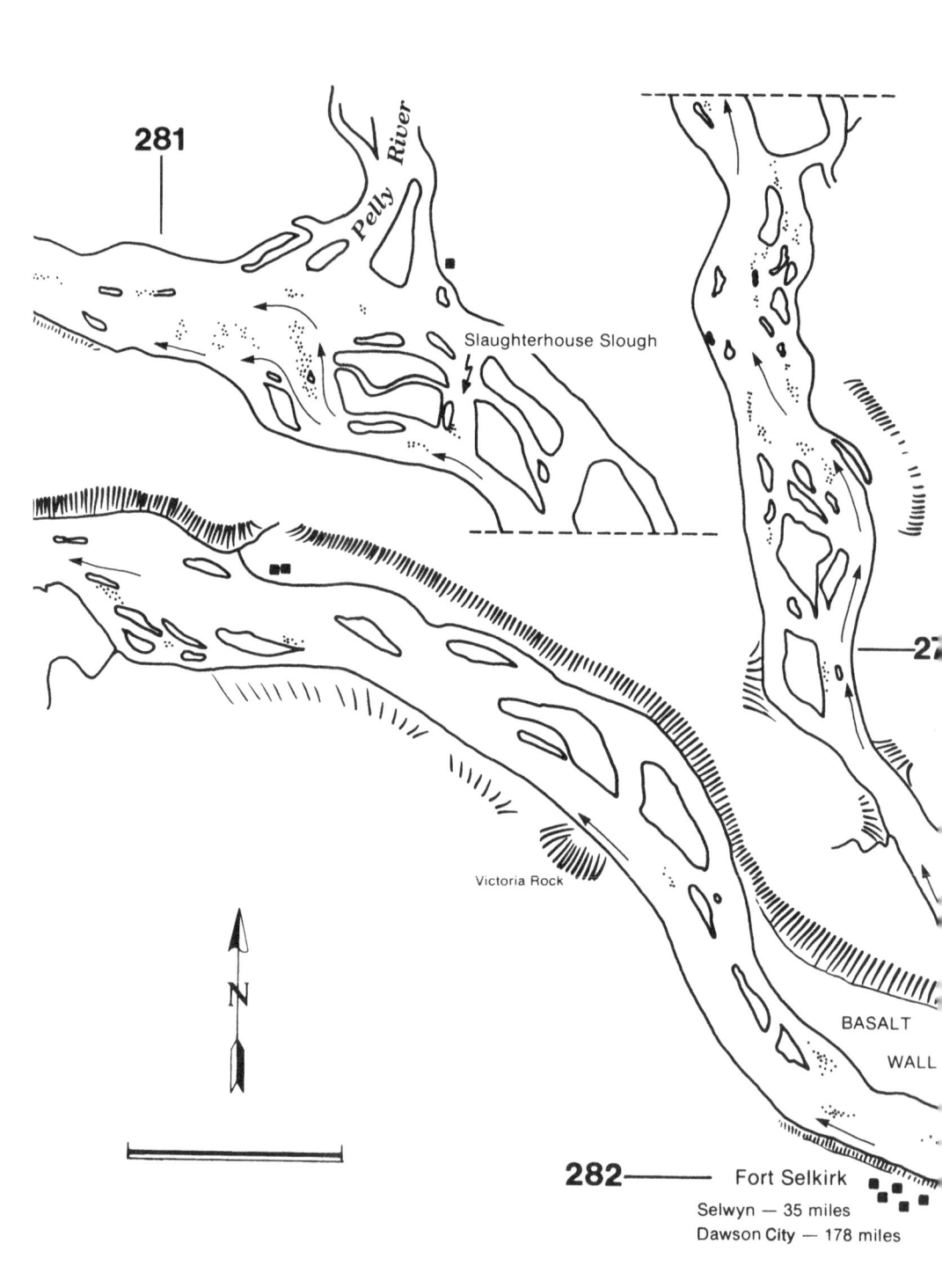

Pelly River

Slaughterhouse Slough

Victoria Rock

N

BASALT WALL

282 — Fort Selkirk
Selwyn — 35 miles
Dawson City — 178 miles

The next afternoon two hunters and their families returned to the post from a hunting trip up the Pelly. Before they could escape, the Chilkats had waded out into the swift water to grab the boat and pull it ashore.

This action seemed to set them off, especially after two Indians working for Campbell disarmed two Chilkats. The battle was on. Several of them rushed Campbell, whose life was saved at the first by two rifles that misfired. There were so many on him that the Indians got in each other's way and could neither shoot nor stab him with their knives.

Inexplicably, when they had wrestled him to the river bank, they released him. He and a few others managed to get into their boats and head downstream to the next Hudson's Bay Company trading post at Fort Yukon. After Campbell's undignified departure the Chilkats burned the post. Then began the most remarkable hike on record. Campbell walked back to Fort Simpson, where the Liard River meets the Mackenzie. He hoped to get permission to reestablish Fort Selkirk, but nobody could

Since this photo was taken, the government has sent in crews to restore the large Indian cemetery at Fort Selkirk.

give him that power. So, in the middle of the winter, he struck out over the mountains on snowshoes to Fort Garry (now Winnipeg, Manitoba) and again was rebuffed. By the time he reached Fort Garry, he had hiked more than 2000 miles (3200 km) across several mountain ranges, including the awesome Rockies. Still determined, he snowshoed on down to Minnesota to board a train to headquarters in Montreal. And all for naught; the company would not honor his request to rebuild Selkirk.

The post lay silent until the Klondike gold rush, when the Canadian government sent a company of the Yukon Field Force to join the RCMP there, and a town grew up around the post. For a while, there was a plan afoot to make Fort Selkirk the capital city of the new Yukon Territory, but Dawson City won out over Selkirk and became the capital.

Selkirk was an important station on the telegraph line that ran between Whitehorse and Dawson City. Some of the poles and insulators stuck into trees can be seen all along the route. At Selkirk, you can see boxes of insulators and pieces of telephones hanging on walls. When the line was in operation, men were stationed along the route and were responsible for its care. Each summer the men would walk along their lines to repair them or clear brush away from them, then catch a steamboat back home.

Fort Selkirk thrived until the 1950s, with about 200 persons living there. Then the highway to Dawson City was built, and the residents moved to the highway: the settlement on the river was abandoned.

The Remains of Old Fort Selkirk

When the people who had lived along the river moved to the highway, most of them left behind their china, stoves, furniture, curtains, drapes and bedding. The freight rates on the steamboats were so high that it was cheaper to leave them and replace everything from stores in Whitehorse and Dawson City.

mile 282

Until the past few years, when boaters started using the river again and helping themselves to what was not theirs, it wasn't unusual to walk into one of the unlocked houses and find tables set as if for company, pots and pans gleaming from their pegs in the kitchen and stoves banked for fire, with more firewood in containers behind the stoves.

Before the coming of recreational boaters from outside the Yukon drainage system, these houses were used by the river people as way stations. The law of the North—that you leave the place clean, replace any food you may have eaten and leave a fire ready to light—remained much in effect. Some removed items from the house and buildings as they were needed, but the unspoken law was strong. That law, unfortunately, is weakening as tourists and other outsiders pass through the territory. Were it not for the efforts of Danny Roberts, there would be little left at Fort Selkirk.

The town that remains consists of the schoolhouse, an Anglican church and minister's home, a Taylor & Drury store, a few sturdy houses and remains of the Yukon Field Force headquarters.

Back in the timber is a Catholic church (which tells you the Anglicans were more powerful there than the Catholics) and the altar appears ready for mass to be celebrated.

One of the most interesting sites around Selkirk is the Indian cemetery near the Catholic church. One of the largest on the river, it has many graves with fences and headstones made of wood carved into unsophisticated but artistic designs.

A typical Yukon River scene: cutbanks on the right where the river swings against the bluff, and sweepers on the left.

Fort Selkirk as it looks late at night during the almost unending daylight of June and July.

Directly across the river from Selkirk is the high, black basalt wall that runs downriver 12 miles (19 km) and up the Pelly 2 or 3 miles (3-4 km), an old lava flow from a long extinct volcano. The top of the wall is decorated with aspen and birch trees, and only an occasional patch of lichen can be seen clinging to the wall itself.

It is said that cannonballs are scattered along its base and the wall itself is pocked from ceremonial cannon shots that were fired from Selkirk.

One further note: The Roberts family moved back to Selkirk, where both Danny and his wife were born and schooled, and they moved there for the privacy it offered. They are friendly people, but like the rest of us they don't appreciate strangers walking around their house and peering in the windows at them. There is something that gives visitors to the North the idea that the local residents, especially if they are Indian (as the Robertses are) or Eskimo, won't mind tourists invading their privacy and taking pictures of them without permission. It is a common ailment, but one which can be healed by asking yourself: Would I mind if someone walked into my yard, peered into my window and took pictures of my family? You might also ask yourself if you would feel any differently about it if the peerers and clickers were of a different race, say Indian or Eskimo . . .

Wind- and rain-carved hillsides above the river.

Fort Selkirk to Stewart Island

The character of the river changes considerably at Selkirk as the low, swampy banks are replaced by cliffs and mountains in the background. Some geologists believe the original river followed the Pelly down to Selkirk and that the present Yukon above Selkirk to the headwater lakes was carved out at the end of the ice age.

As you leave Selkirk you will be confronted with the canyon. A good deal of time will be spent looking almost straight up to see over the top of the 12-mile-long (19-km) basalt wall on the right (north) shore. The river cuts directly into the base of the cliffs, which rise 140 meters or more. Landing sites on that side are few. The main channel hugs the cliffs for the most part, and the cliffs extend 12 miles (19 km) downstream to a place called Twin Falls. Apparently two waterfalls are formed there during spring melt, but they don't flow during the summer. All you can hope to see in summer are twin stains on the cliff.

mile 295

Camps, Way Stations and Creeks Below Selkirk

There are many old woodcutters' camps and way stations along this stretch of river. Isaac Creek was the site of both a placer mine and a woodcutters' camp, although the buildings have been demolished. Britannia Creek has an old road that ran up into the mountains nearly 25 miles (40 km) to a placer mine. Ballarat Creek has cabins in good repair, privately owned.

Coffee Creek was an old trading post that also has buildings, usually occupied now. A trail leading up from Coffee Creek into the mountains was used as a route to the Chisana Gold Rush in Alaska in 1913. Since the trail hasn't been used in decades, it is

mile 345

Twin Falls

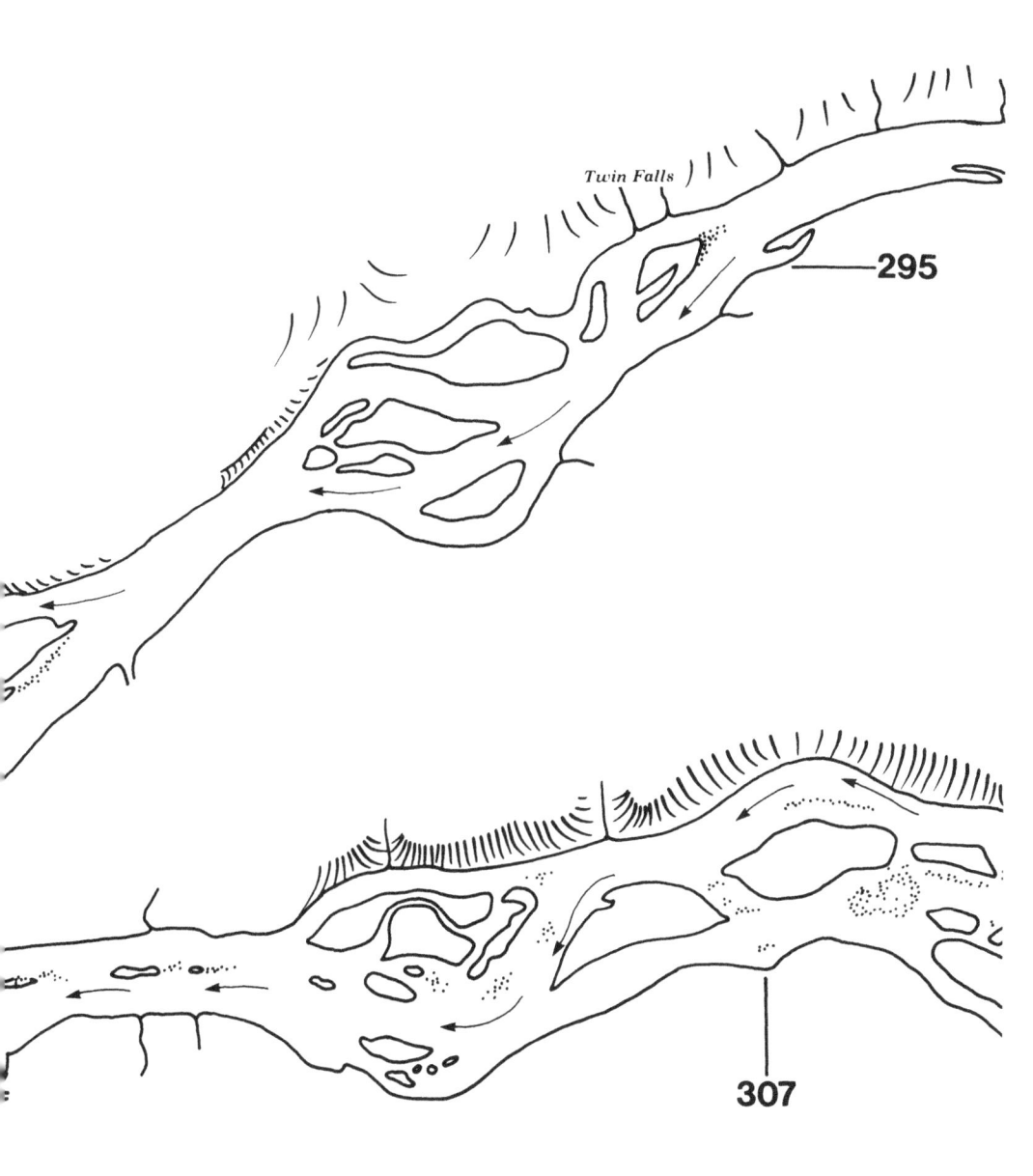

—295

307

mostly grown over now. A few of the cabins are used during winters by trappers. Most are at the head of trails or wagon roads inland, which make good short hikes. Kirkman Creek, a former post office and small farm, is privately owned and maintained.

One should avoid using privately owned cabins. There are adequate public campsites. In the case of Kirkman Creek, the hayfield behind the house is a good campsite.

Black Creek

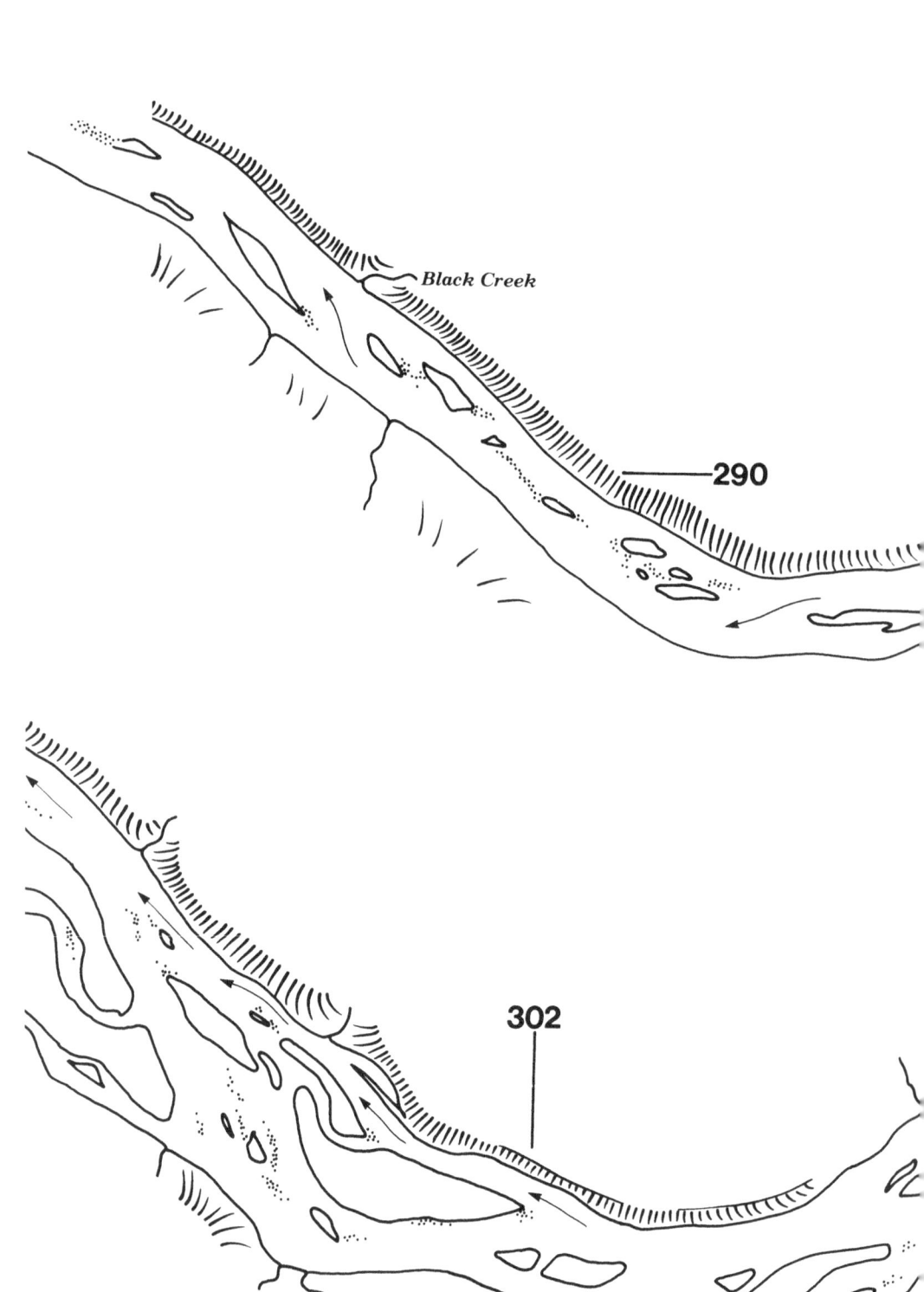

290

302

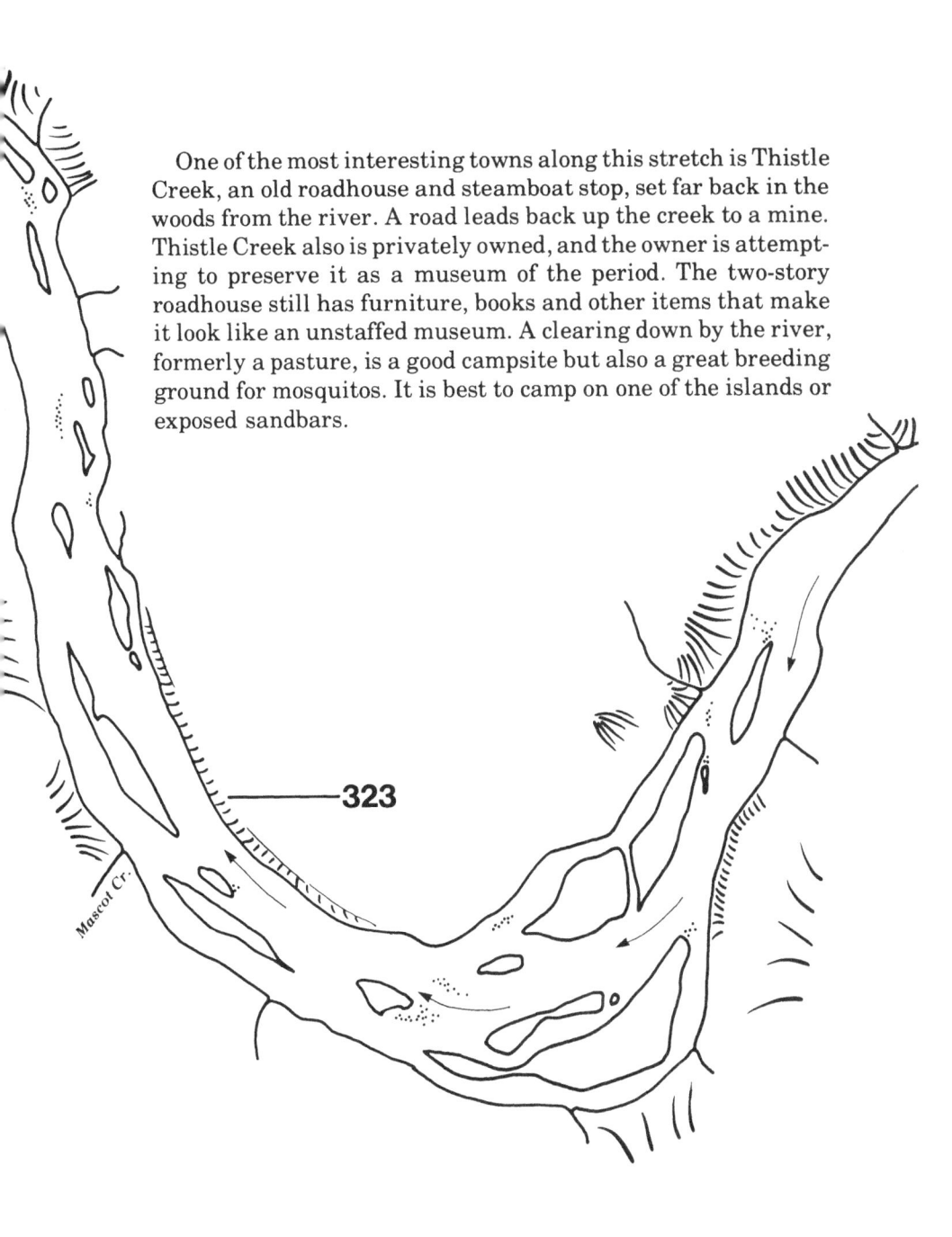

One of the most interesting towns along this stretch is Thistle Creek, an old roadhouse and steamboat stop, set far back in the woods from the river. A road leads back up the creek to a mine. Thistle Creek also is privately owned, and the owner is attempting to preserve it as a museum of the period. The two-story roadhouse still has furniture, books and other items that make it look like an unstaffed museum. A clearing down by the river, formerly a pasture, is a good campsite but also a great breeding ground for mosquitos. It is best to camp on one of the islands or exposed sandbars.

317
Selwyn Station
Selwyn River

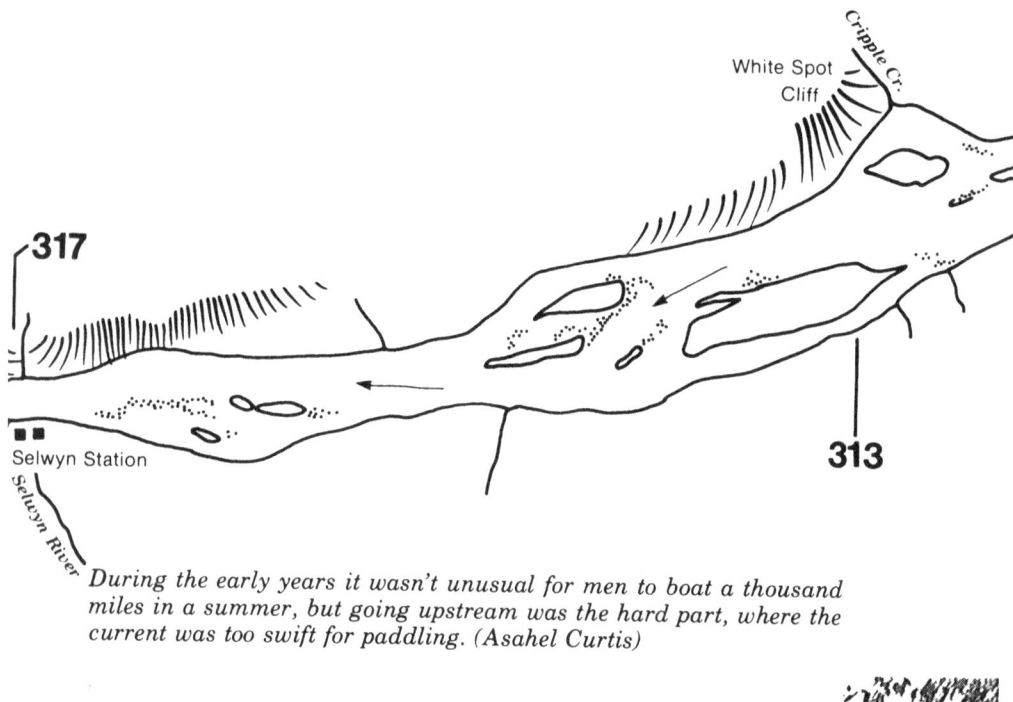

White Spot Cliff
Cripple Cr.

313

During the early years it wasn't unusual for men to boat a thousand miles in a summer, but going upstream was the hard part, where the current was too swift for paddling. (Asahel Curtis)

335

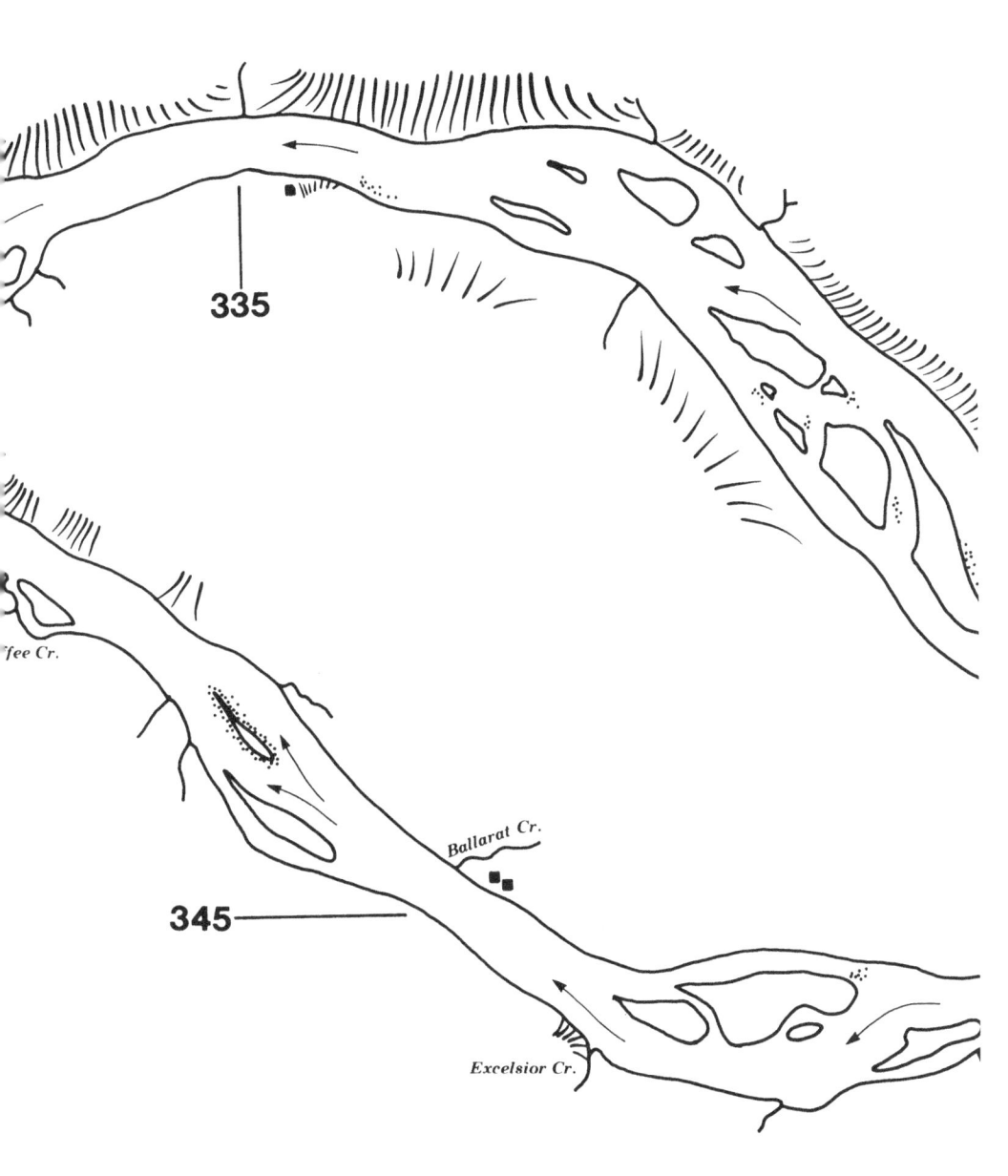

fee Cr.

Ballarat Cr.

345

Excelsior Cr.

98

ew miles beyond Thistle Creek the river becomes grayer as **White River**
the White River enters with its massive load of silt from the St.
Elias Range. The big river adds considerably to the Yukon
River's load; the Yukon becomes more than a mile wide for most
of the rest of the trip. It is best to fill canteens and jugs from the
side streams from here to Dawson City, although many people
do drink the river water after letting the dirt settle to the
bottom.

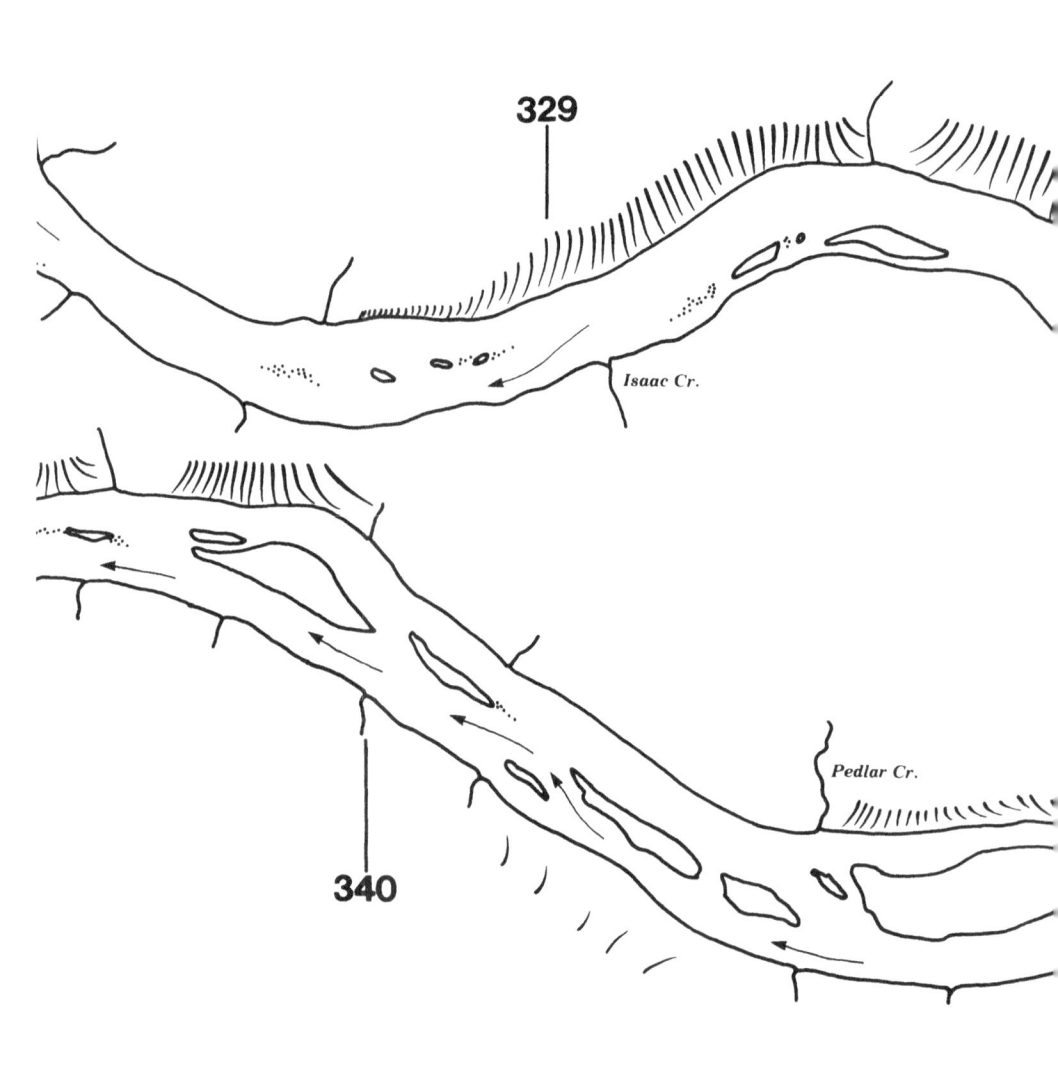

Dan Man Cr.

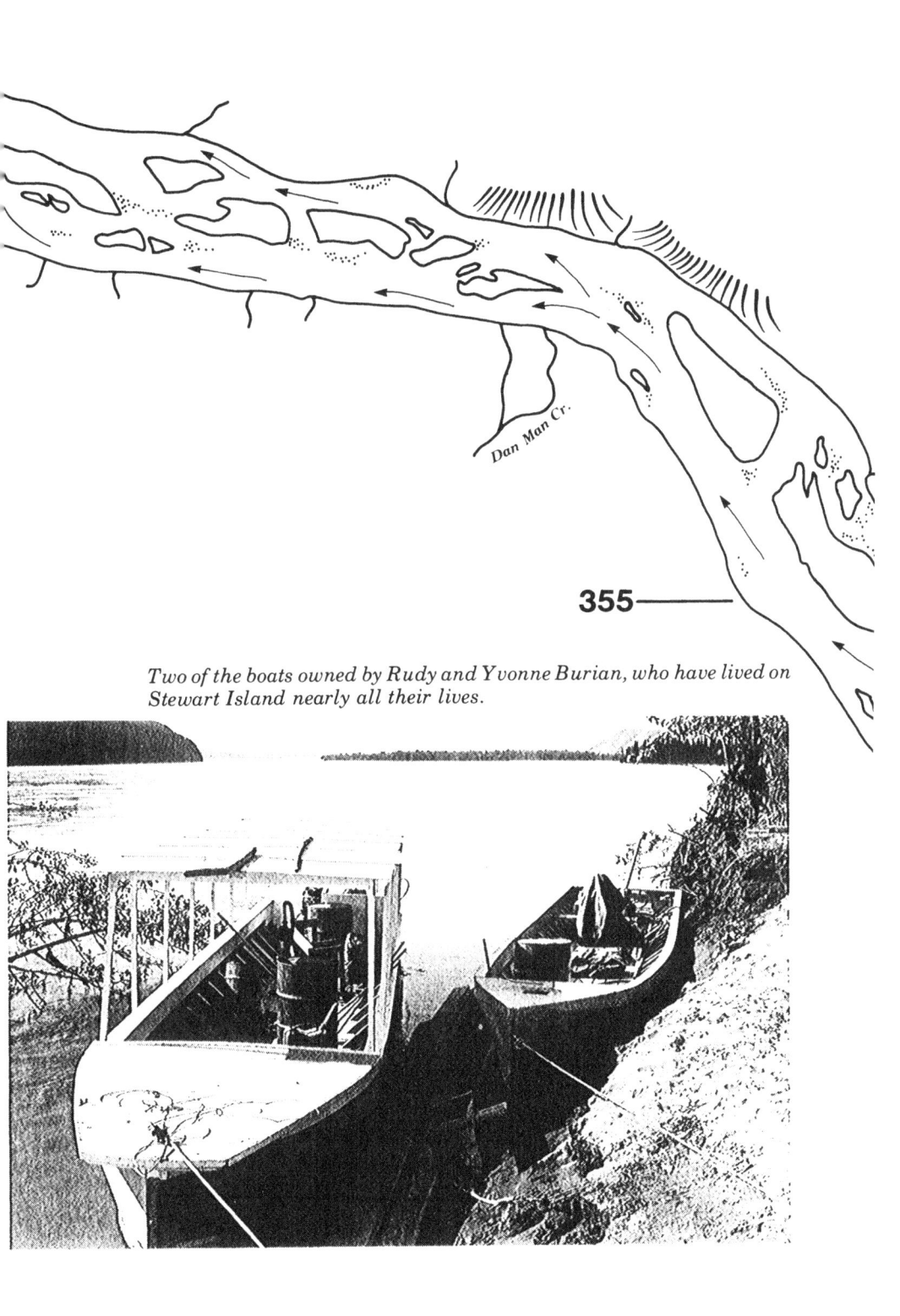

355

Two of the boats owned by Rudy and Yvonne Burian, who have lived on Stewart Island nearly all their lives.

en miles (16 km) from the White River's entrance is Stewart Island, at the mouth of the Stewart River. Rudi and Yvonne Burian have lived on the island most of their lives, and they operate a small store that has been in existence since the gold rush. In addition to the store, they have built several small rental cabins with everything provided except bedding. The Burians are very knowledgeable on the Yukon and its history, and a stop to visit with them should definitely be on the itinerary.

Stewart Island mile 390

The island has been victimized by the Yukon, and nearly every spring the river carves off a big chunk of the island and washes it away.

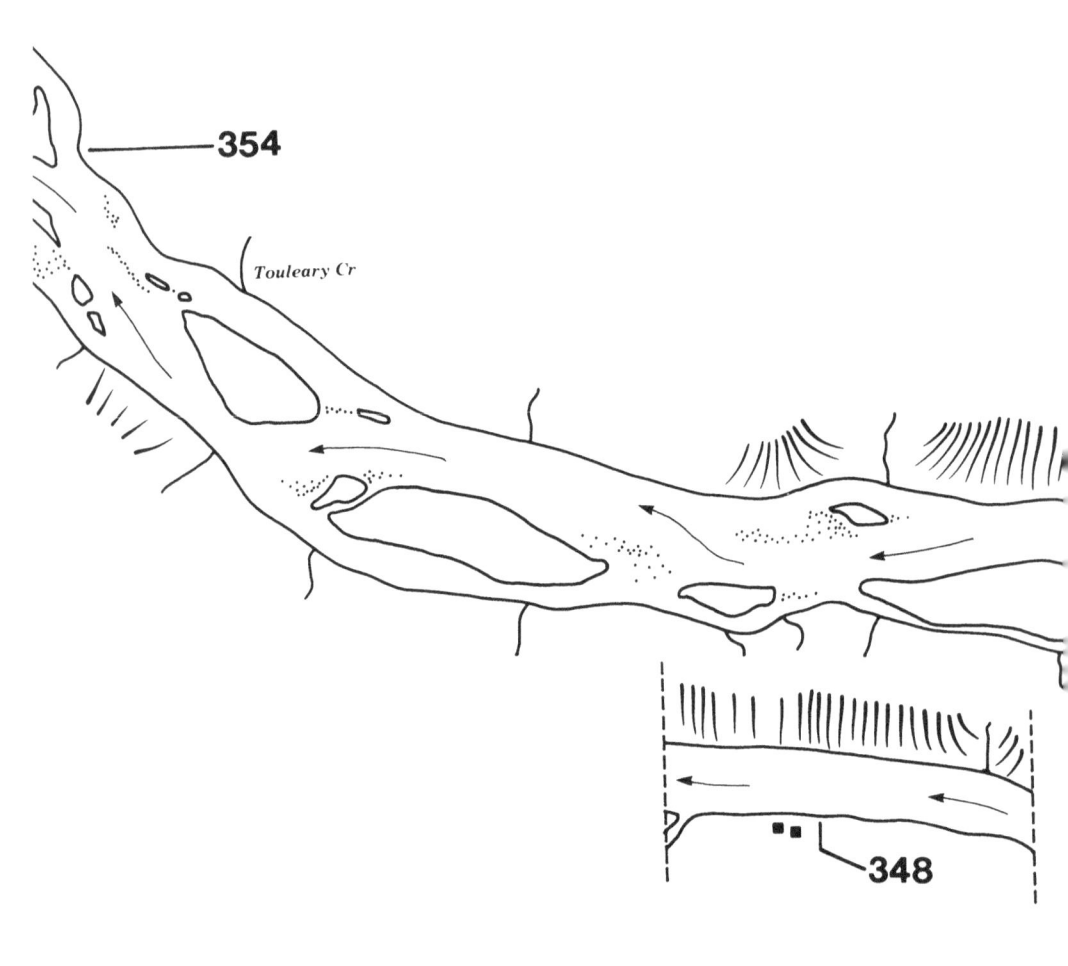

354

Touleary Cr

348

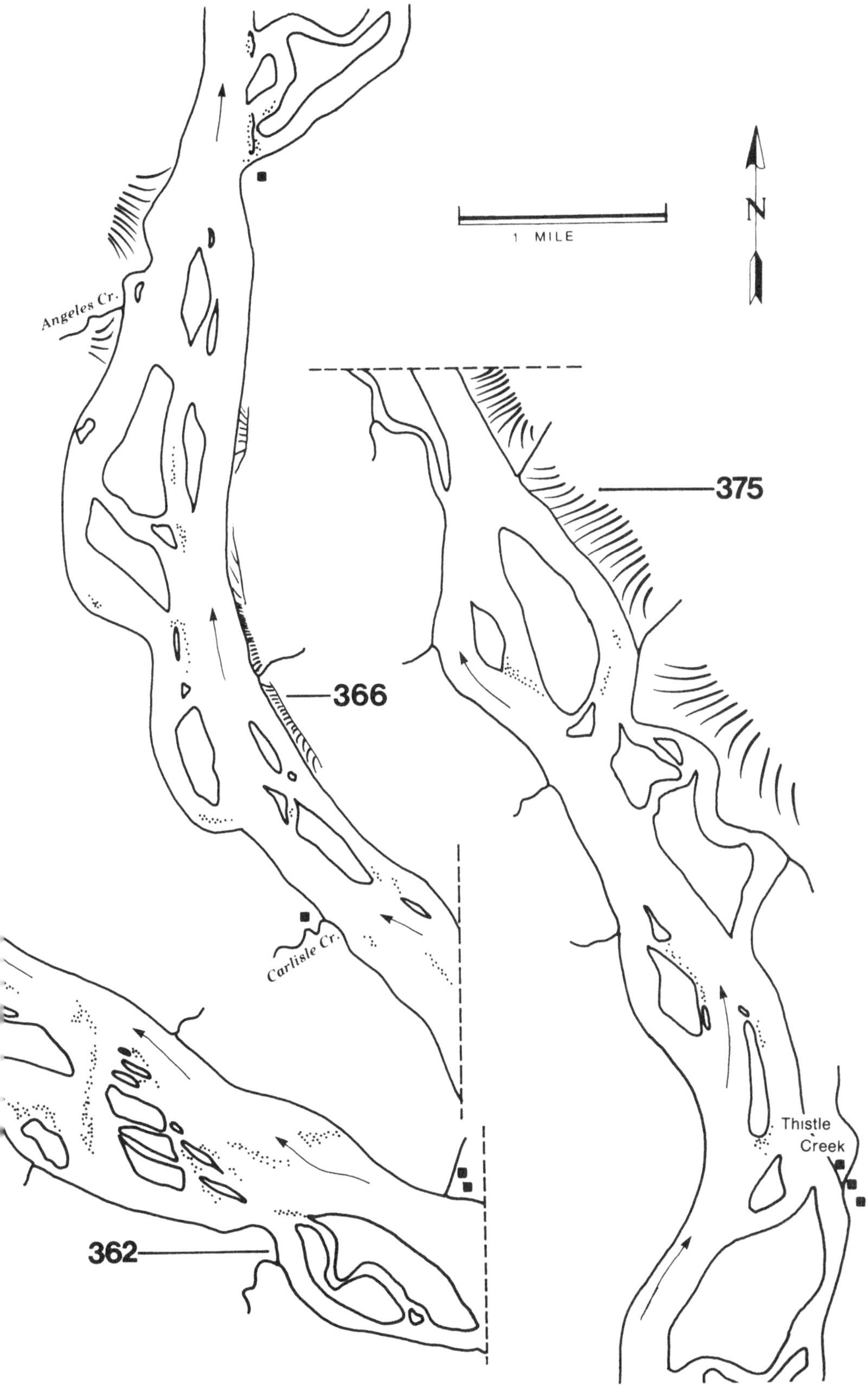

1 MILE
N
Angeles Cr.
375
366
Carlisle Cr.
362
Thistle
Creek

The store has only a few items, such as refreshments and basic food needs, but a candy bar and bottle of cold pop can be a welcome combination after a few hot days on the river. Occasionally the Burians will have pelts for sale, such as ermine and fox, since they trap during the winter.

They also have a small museum near the store with artifacts they've picked up along the Stewart and Yukon, including a large selection of rare bottles.

A visit with the Burians also prepares you for your reentry into civilization. They live 70 miles (113 km) from the nearest town (Dawson City), but they have a broad, grassy lawn they keep mowed, and during nice weather they sit outside in lawn chairs and watch the river flow past. The Burians dispel many of the images we have of the Far North, of people living in cabins with dirt floors and of being away from civilization so long they forget how to talk.

During the gold rush, smart businessmen invested in food items, such as cattle, instead of in mining claims. (Asahel Curtis)

The Stewart River had a small gold rush on it that was overshadowed by the Klondike strike. Later, Stewart Island was an important barge terminal when steamboats ran the Stewart delivering goods to the mine at Mayo and hauling ore downstream.

Jack London wintered over on the Stewart River in 1898-99, and things he saw and heard that winter resulted in many of his famous, if exaggerated, stories.

Late evening–about 10 p.m.–on the river.

Frisco Cr.

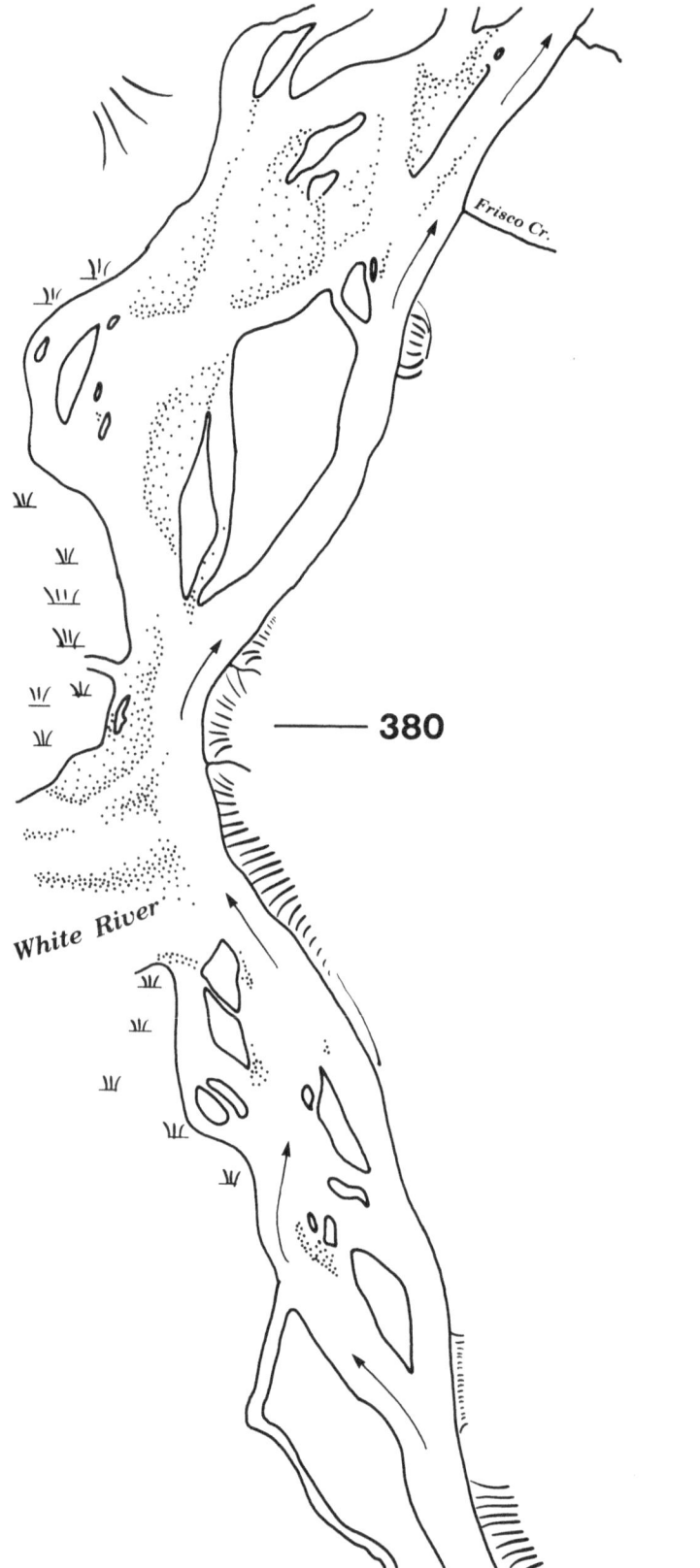

380

White River

A freighter canoe and dock downstream from Dawson City at the abandoned Indian village of Moosehide.

Stewart Island to Dawson City

Numerous campsites with good supplies of firewood can be found almost at will along the river between Stewart Island and Dawson City.

Some boaters have found it a boon to their morale to go up the Sixtymile River a short distance and camp the last night before entering Dawson City. The Sixtymile isn't as cold as the Yukon and hardy travelers can bathe in it without undue discomfort.

Sixtymile River

Directly across from the mouth of the Sixtymile River is one of the river's more important historic spots. Variously called Sixtymile Island and Ogilvie Post, it was here the first post office in the Yukon was built. Joe LaDue, the trader who operated the post, became the founder of Dawson City when he abandoned Ogilvie Post and headed downstream to start a new town. In the process, he became a wealthy man, operating a sawmill and selling off business lots. Several cabins remain at Ogilvie Post in various stages of decay.

This is the last day on the river for most boaters, and you know the trip is over when you see a bald spot on a mountainside ahead. That is the slide scar that marks Dawson City; it has been a beacon for boaters on the river since the 1890s. The scar is called Moosehide; and an Indian village three miles (five km) downstream has the same name. According to Indian oral history, the slide covered a village there centuries ago when Indians from another tribe caused the slide to cover their enemy's campsite.

396

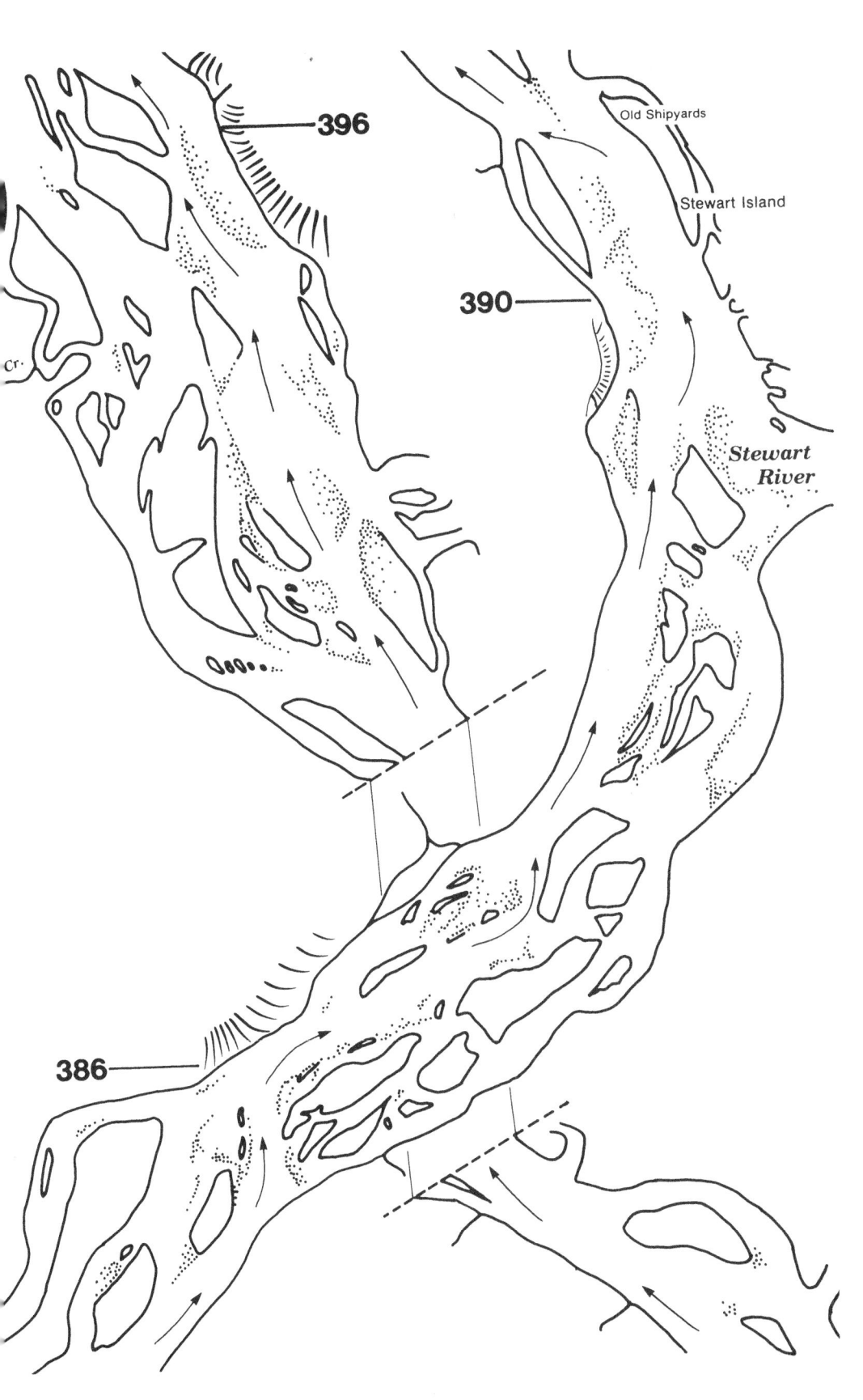

390

Old Shipyards

Stewart Island

Stewart River

386

Klondike River

On the approach to Dawson City, boaters have to cut across the current of the Klondike River as it enters the Yukon; it creates a backwater the steamboats used to get to shore. The best place to land is in the vicinity of the old paddlewheeler *Keno*, now a museum on the bank. This is in the heart of town and you'll have a shorter distance to carry your gear from the river to hotels.

Restrain yourself from bragging to locals that you just came down the river in a boat, all the way from headwaters. They won't be impressed, because they've done it numerous times, their parents did it and hundreds of people do it each year. Tourists will be more easily impressed—may even want to take a picture of you. Don't smile. Look ominous.

Dawson City

mile 460

Dawson City has been described by many writers as an eccentric little town. Perhaps individualistic would be a kinder word, because it is definitely not your usual small town. With its colorful history and its knack of attracting strong personalities for permanent residents, you sometimes will have the feeling you've stepped off the river onto a movie set.

Until the end of the steamboat era, Dawson City was the major city in the Yukon and the territorial capital. The old Commissioner's Residence still stands in good repair at the upriver edge of town. The government was moved to Whitehorse in 1953, so the residence stands vacant. After the government left, the town's population dwindled and the vacated homes and cabins became targets for vandals.

During the past few years, Dawson City has become more and more like a live-in museum. The Canadian government has budgeted several million dollars for restoration and preservation, and several of the old swaybacked buildings that might have soon fallen in on themselves have been jacked up and had new foundations installed to avoid the uncertainties of building on permafrost. Buildings in Dawson City now are built either on high pads of gravel or on steel pilings driven deep into the ground.

N

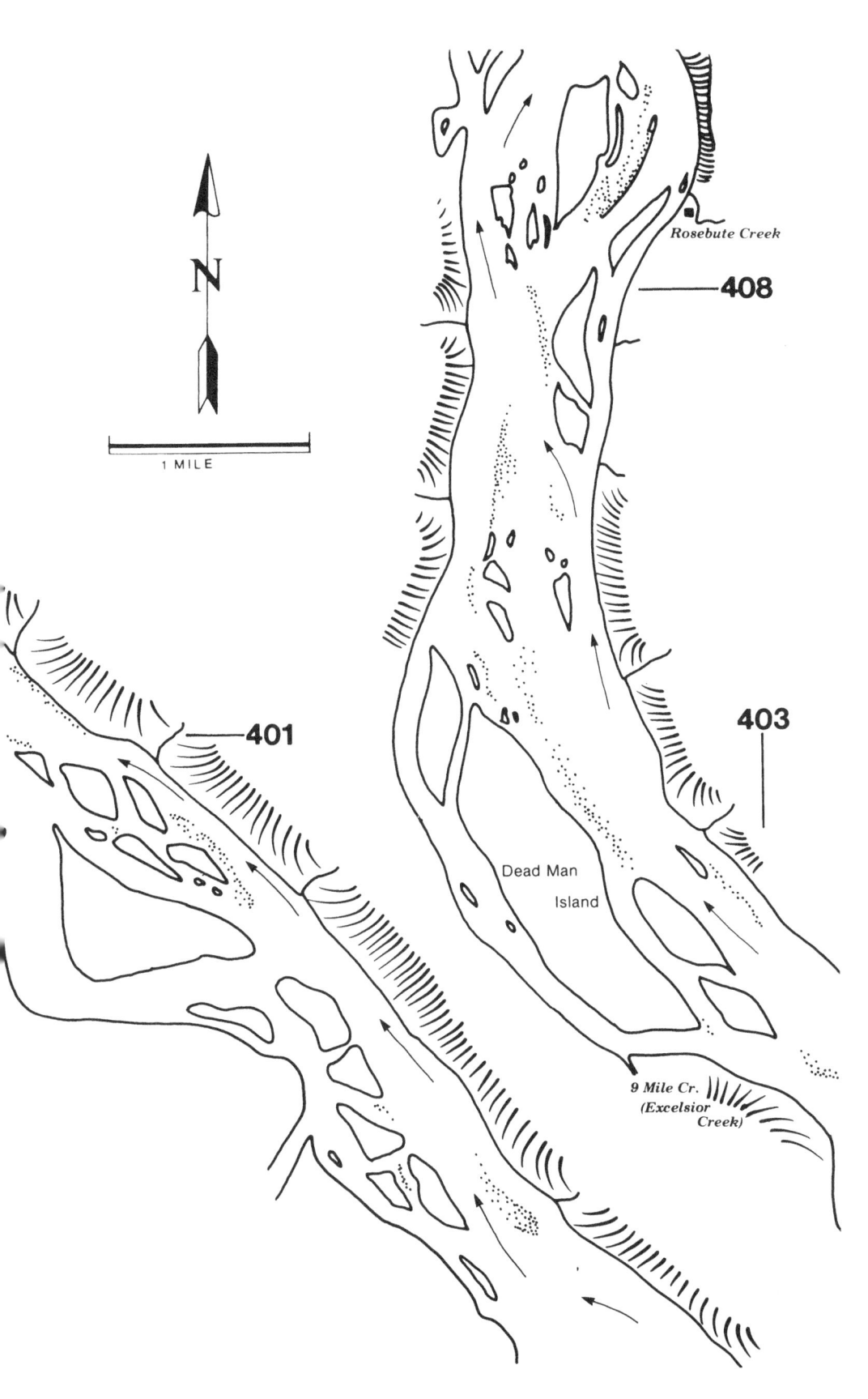

1 MILE

401

408

Rosebute Creek

403

Dead Man Island

9 Mile Cr. (Excelsior Creek)

The town's showplace is the Palace Grand Theater, where performances of musical comedy and English music hall-type reviews are given during the summer months. The theater originally was built by Arizona Charlie Meadows during the Klondike heyday, burned, rebuilt and then allowed to fall into a state of disrepair after the population dwindled. In 1960 the Klondike Visitors Association bought it and turned it over to the federal government the following year for restoration to its 1899 appearance. The theater is open during the day for tours and photographs.

The restored Palace Grand Theater at left is the showpiece of Dawson City. A firebreak to protect the city from frequent lightning-caused forest fires shows on the hillside above.

Lucky Joe Cr.

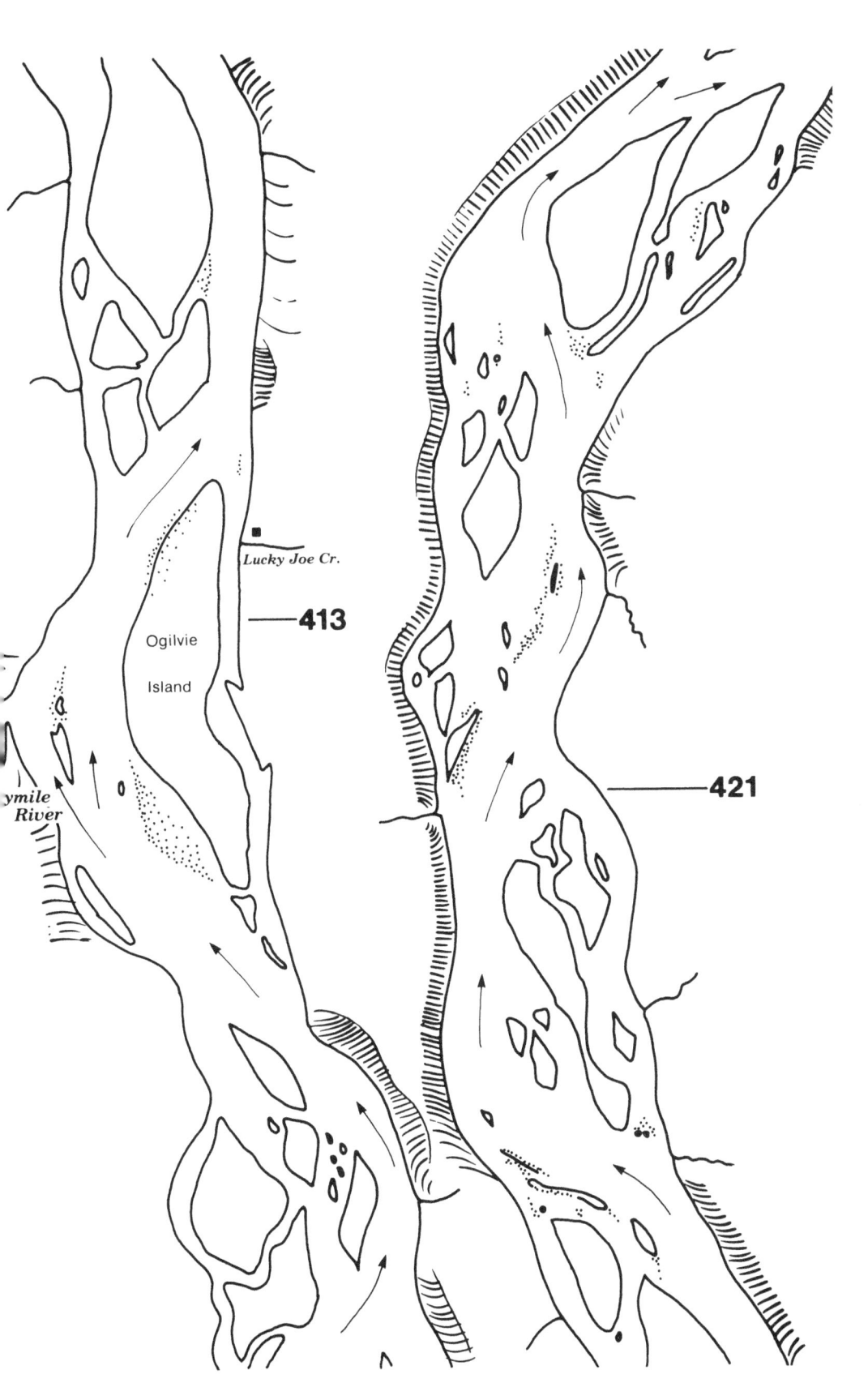

413

Ogilvie Island

ymile River

421

428

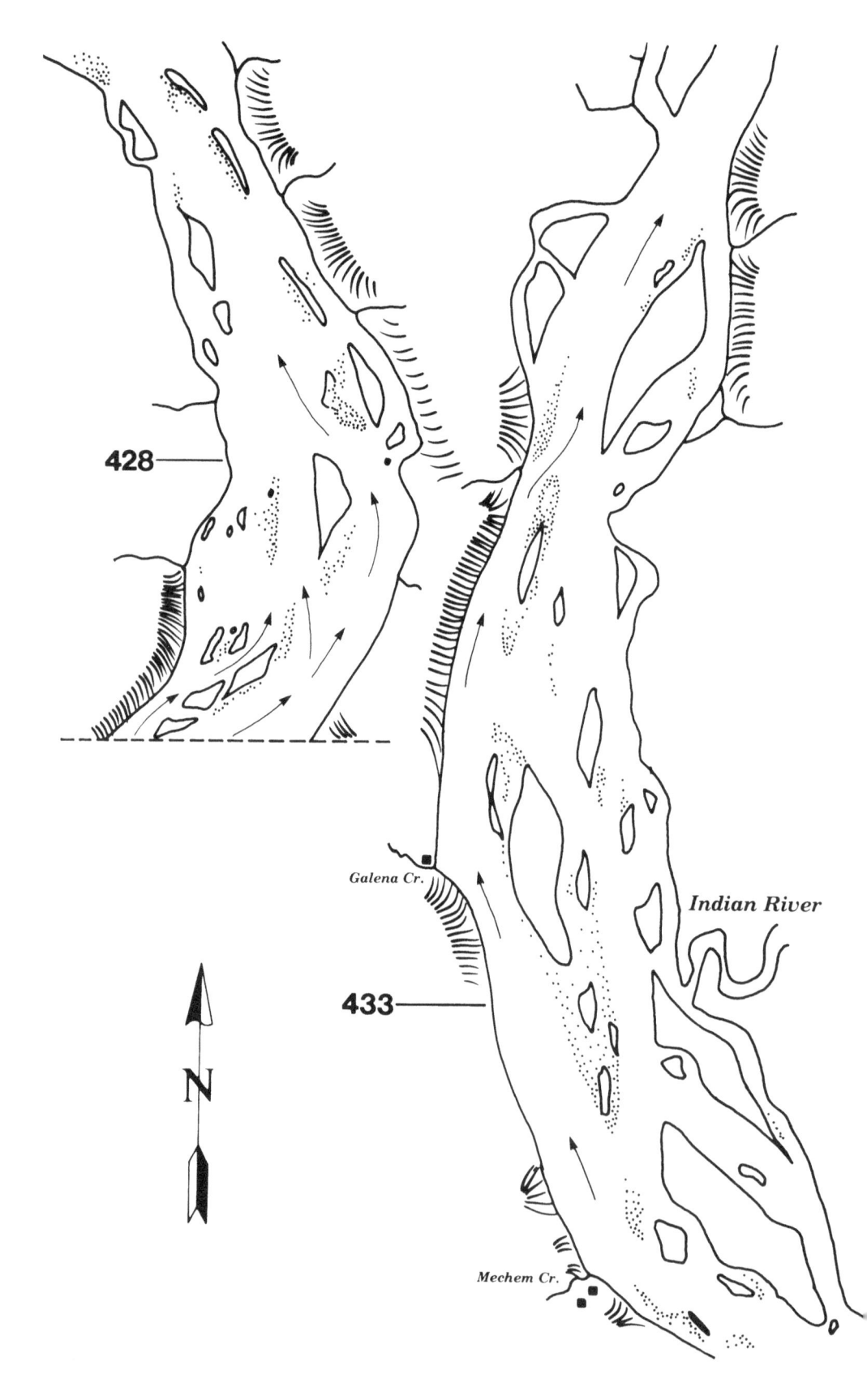

433

N

Galena Cr.

Indian River

Mechem Cr.

ner Cr.

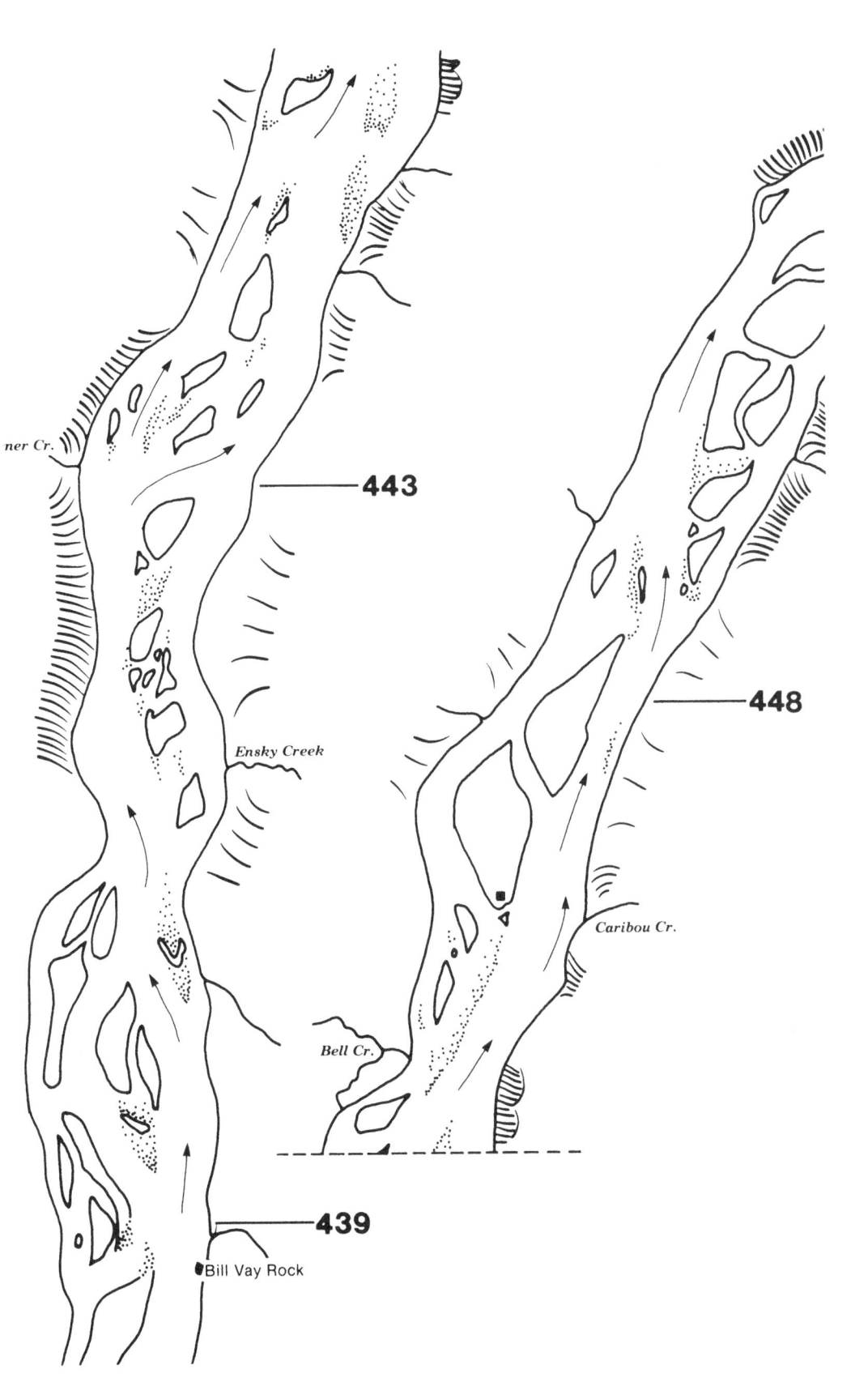

443

Ensky Creek

448

Caribou Cr.

Bell Cr.

439

Bill Vay Rock

There is an automobile campground in town, but those tent camping should plan on going across the Yukon River to set up their tents. This avoids whatever problem with vandalism and theft may exist in town. A free ferry runs back and forth across the river and docks downstream a short distance from the *Keno*. There are public showers and a laundromat at the Northwestern Motel.

Among the other attractions in town are Robert Service's cabin at Eighth and Church streets, where readings of his poetry are given during the afternoons in summer; the "Gold Room" in the top floor of the Bank of Commerce on the river bank, where various measuring and weighing devices are exhibited; half of Jack London's cabin (the other half was hauled to Jack London Square in Oakland, California); or simply strolling around town taking in the sights.

Some maps still show Klondike City, which locals call Lousetown, on the opposite side of the Klondike River. Nearly everything is gone now and it is hardly worth the effort to go over there. The settlement became the red-light district for Dawson City, and clients traveled back and forth on a rickety footbridge, which made it difficult for men to consort with the ladies over there without being seen by someone.

Since you have followed the Trail of '98 to the Klondike, a visit to the goldfields should be considered part of the package. And it is much better to go on a guided tour than to rent a car and go out without benefit of a guide.

Today, about all that remains of the original stampede is the long, curving piles of dredge tailings left behind the Guggenheim-owned dredges that followed the first miners. Bonanza Creek, where the discovery was made, is reached by driving along a road built atop the dredge tailings, and you pass the dredge that did the damage—a huge, four-story monster that cranked and groaned and whistled while turning out a pitifully small-looking stream of gold. Old-timers say that watching one of the dredges work was like watching a carnival; they were so huge, so noisy, yet went to all that work to turn out something measured in ounces rather than tons.

If you should arrive in Dawson City toward the longest day of the year—June 22—you will want to join the stampede to the top of Midnight Dome overlooking Dawson City and the river. It

460

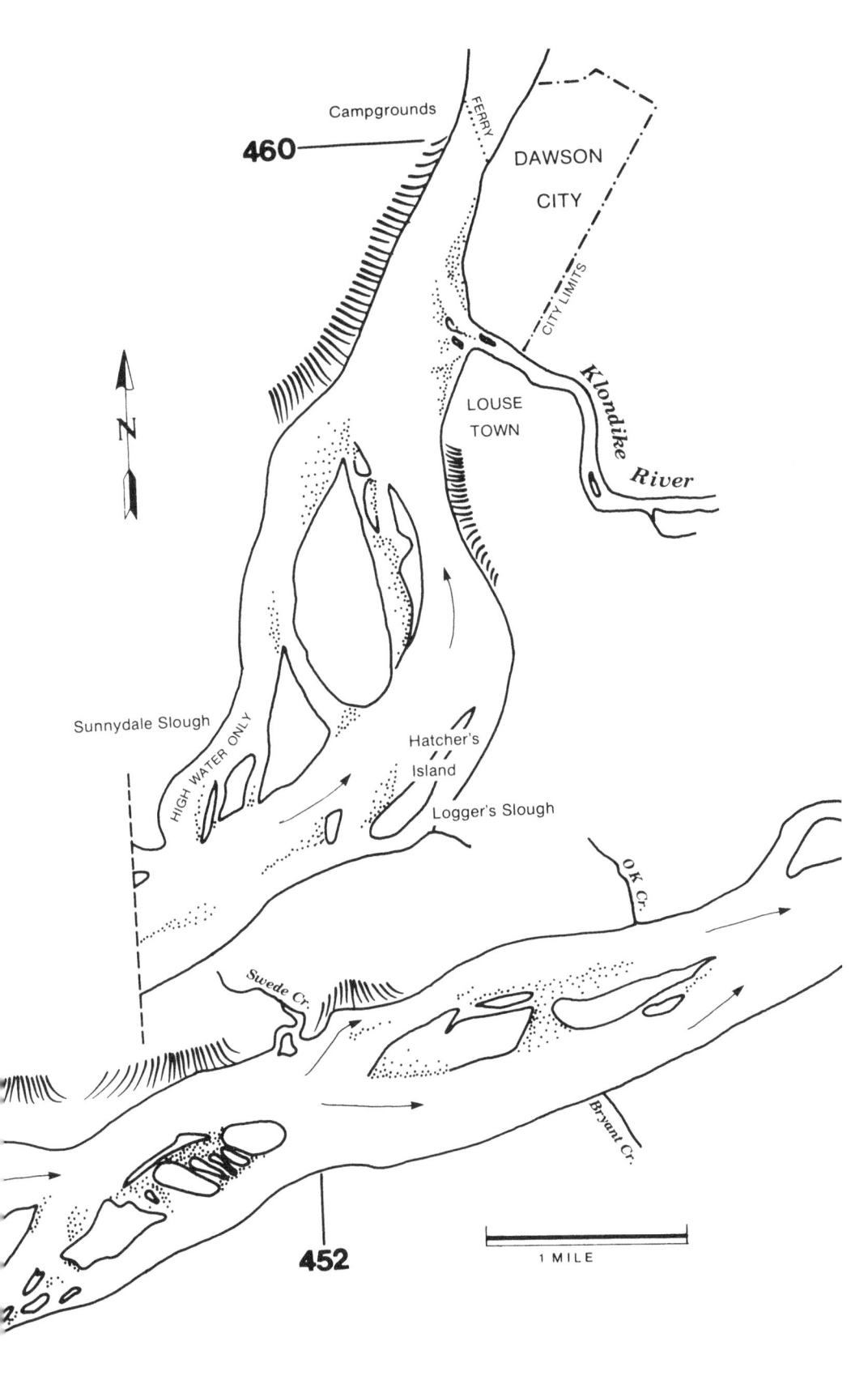

Campgrounds

FERRY

DAWSON CITY

CITY LIMITS

Klondike River

LOUSE TOWN

N

Sunnydale Slough

HIGH WATER ONLY

Hatcher's Island

Logger's Slough

O K Cr.

Swede Cr.

Bryant Cr.

452

1 MILE

is a tradition that most Dawsonites observe and big parties are sometimes held up there. Back in town, a baseball game starts at midnight each year with no playing field lights necessary.

A good hike from Dawson City can be made along the face of the slide scar and down a trail to Moosehide, the abandoned Indian village. A tour boat runs the same route several times a day, but most people who have spent two weeks in a boat prefer walking. The trail climbs to the top of the high cliffs overlooking the river, then drops back down again to the wide valley occupied by Moosehide. The town is where most Indians in the area lived, but over the years they moved into Dawson City for mining and service industry jobs, and eventually abandoned the town entirely.

The Anglican church had a mission there with a church, a school and teachers' quarters. Most of the church furniture is still intact, including a pump organ that works and hymn books. The school building still has the desks and some furniture, and the teachers' quarters upstairs appear almost ready to move into.

You can make arrangements with the tour boat operator to ride down to the village and walk back, or vice versa.

Lousetown in its heyday; only brush remains. (Asahel Curtis)

Danny Roberts, who has been caretaker of Fort Selkirk for some 20 years, was born and reared on the river during the steamboat era. He and his wife returned to the area because they like the solitude.

Tributary Rivers

Many canoeists and kayakers prefer to avoid the busy Yukon River and lake system by taking trips down the tributary streams that flow into the Yukon between Lake Laberge and Dawson City. The major navigable rivers are the Teslin, Big Salmon, Pelly, Macmillan, White, Stewart and Sixtymile rivers.

Brief summaries of those rivers which follow are taken from a series of wild river surveys made in 1971 by four-man canoe teams sponsored by the Department of Indian Affairs and Northern Development, National and Historic Parks Branch. Leader of the survey was Ian Donaldson, who wrote the reports and made them available to the public. Copies are available through the Travel and Information Branch, Yukon Territorial Government, Box 2703, Whitehorse, Y.T.

Since these rivers are more remote and less traveled than the Yukon and the lake system, it cannot be overemphasized that only experienced canoeists or kayakers should attempt them, and that safety precautions should be taken at all times.

The author has not traveled on these tributary rivers, but he can attest to the accuracy and conclusions of Donaldson's reports on the Yukon River and its headwater lakes.

Teslin River

Access You can enter the water either at the town of Teslin on Lake Teslin, or, to bypass the lake, at Johnson's Crossing on the Teslin River.

Mileage Donaldson's crew traveled the 260 miles (418 km) from Teslin to Carmacks in 13 days.

Historical Significance This route was used by some gold rushers who came up the Inside Passage to Wrangell, Alaska, then up the Stikine River to Telegraph Creek, B.C., then overland to Teslin Lake. A steamboat service operated three years on the lake and river, which resulted in the founding of Teslin, Johnson's Crossing, M'Clintock, Teslin Crossing, Mason Landing and Hootalinqua, all of which are ghost towns today.

A telegraph line was built between Telegraph Creek and Hootalinqua, where it linked to the wire down the Yukon River and back over White Pass to Skagway.

Navigation The Teslin presents no difficulty for experienced boaters. There are a few sets of rapids, particularly in the Boswell Creek area and Roaring Bull Rapids, but they are not rated as dangerous. It is recommended, however, that all rapids be scouted on foot before entering.

Big Salmon River

Access Quiet Lake on the Canol Road, 45 miles (74 km) from Johnson's Crossing.

Mileage Approximately 247 miles (397 km) from the southern end of Quiet Lake to Carmacks; 10 days.

River Character Little historical significance, but noted for its wilderness character. No pollution in the river and no man-made structures are found until the Yukon River is reached.

Navigation Quiet Lake is connected to Sandy Lake by a shallow, swift stream that is bordered by willows which make landings difficult. The banks of the Big Salmon are frequently lined with sweepers which constitute a hazard. Other banks range upward to 23 meters high, also making landings difficult. There are numerous rapids on the river varying from one hundred feet to more than a thousand feet long. Fortunately, it is possible to pull out for scouting before entering most rapids. Some may present problems during low-water periods due to boulders and bars. Portaging would involve brush-beating through dense undergrowth.

A whirlpool occurs at the junction of the Big Salmon and South Big Salmon rivers with a vortex about a foot deep and five to six feet wide. It can be avoided by following the right limit of the Big Salmon.

Pelly River

Ross River, Mile 138 (km 222) Canol Road. **Access**

249 miles (400 km) from Ross River to Fort Selkirk, Yukon River; eight days. **Mileage**

Robert Campbell, the Hudson's Bay Company explorer and trader, traveled down the Pelly in 1840 and founded Fort Pelly Banks at the junction of Campbell Creek and the Pelly, and later Fort Selkirk where the Pelly enters the Yukon. In 1898 George M. Dawson followed the same route for the Geological Survey of Canada and wrote one of the most literate reports ever composed on what then was called the Yukon district. **Historical Significance**

Today the river is still largely untouched by civilization outside the towns of Ross River and Pelly Crossing. You have the choice of leaving the river at Pelly Crossing on the Dawson Highway, or continuing to Fort Selkirk and downriver to Dawson City.

There are three sets of rapids between the Faro Bridge and Pelly Crossing which the skilled canoeist will find no difficulty navigating: Little and Big Fishhook Rapids and the rapids in Granite Canyon. They may pose problems during periods of high water, and should definitely be scouted. Both Big and Little Fishhook Rapids are rated low difficulty at low water and medium at high water. Granite Canyon is rated low difficulty at the entrance and more difficult farther into the canyon, again depending on the water level. The easiest course is along the right limit, and scouting is required. **Navigation**

Donaldson broke the trip down into three stages in his report.

Ross River to Faro—43 miles (69 km), one day's travel, no rapids.

Faro to Pelly Crossing—163 miles (262 km), two days, medium difficulty rapids.

Pelly Crossing to Fork Selkirk—43 miles (69 km), one day, no rapids.

These unidentified stampeders were typical of the men who went North after gold. (Yukon Archives photo)

Macmillan River

Access This is the most remote of the Yukon tributaries, and access is either up the unimproved Canol Road with four-wheel drive vehicles or by charter aircraft. The Canol crosses the upper river approximately 60 miles (97 km) beyond Ross River.

Mileage Donaldson's crew entered the river at Russell Creek a few miles below the Canol Road and traveled 145 miles (233 km) to the mouth of the river where it empties into the Pelly.

River Character It is the most remote and one of the most beautiful rivers in the Yukon Territory. Surrounded by mountains and dense forests, it also has one of the highest wildlife populations.

Navigation There are no major rapids on the river, with the major difficulties being log jams and sweepers, both of which are easy to avoid. The overall rating of the river is low difficulty, although those entering the river from the Canol Road are encouraged to seek information locally, since Donaldson did not survey it.

Children play with a snow rake used to remove heavy buildup in winter before the weight breaks down the cabin roofs.

White River

Access This is the least interesting river of all those surveyed, one generally described as not worth the effort. It is heavily laden with silt from the St. Elias Range, and it flows through generally uninteresting topography. However, for those who insist, it is accessible from the town of Snag, 17 miles (27 km) off the Alaska Highway at Mile 1188 (Km 1913).

Mileage Eight days for the 180 miles (290 km) to Dawson City (the White enters the Yukon 80 miles (129 km) from Dawson City).

River Character It is one of the major tributaries of the Yukon and was used as a main route from the Yukon to the Chisana gold rush in Alaska in 1913. A pack train service operated between Coffee Creek and Chisana for a short time. The milky river is characterized by swift (average is 4 knots) water, often choppy, with back eddies and frequent sweepers and log jams. The water is not potable due to the high silt content; side streams should be used for drinking. As if the other undesirable characteristics were not enough, the river banks have a number of discarded oil drums and other debris.

Men work a claim on Gold Hill. (Asahel Curtis)

The paddlewheeler Keno *was the first riverboat restored by the Canadian government. It is open daily for guided tours.*

Stewart River

The access from a road is at Mayo, although Donaldson went by plane to the headwaters at Beaver Creek.	**Access**
Two weeks to Dawson City, which includes one day from Stewart Island to Dawson City.	**Mileage**
The roughest part of the river is between Beaver Creek and the town of Mayo, and those interested in chartering a plane to that area should obtain a copy of Donaldson's report. For the purposes of this book, the description will be limited to that part of the river easily accessible by highway. Suffice it to say that the upper river involves portaging around waterfalls and especially rough sets of rapids, and should not be attempted by novices.	**River Character**

Below Mayo the river is not potable and the highway follows it closely until just below Stewart Crossing on the main highway. The stretch along here is the least interesting of the entire river. Most canoeists will prefer putting into the water at Stewart Crossing and continuing down to the Yukon River. Below the crossing, the valley narrows for a few miles, then widens again with islands and sloughs being formed. A few cabins can be seen and evidence of the major gold rush there in the 1890s. Most are protected by the territorial government, including the Maisy May Ranch that was used as a hay ranch to supply the horse-powered transport on the winter road between Dawson City and Whitehorse.

An aerial view of the Klondike valley shows the giant worms of gravel left behind the dredges that came into use after the main gold rush was over. These are referred to as tailings.

Dawson City from Midnight Dome. The Klondike River comes in from the left just above town. (Yukon Government photo)

Sixtymile River

Access The river is reached by turning off the so-called Top of the World Highway that connects Dawson City to the Alaska Highway. The turnoff is 55 miles (89 km) west of Dawson City and 20 miles (32 km) west of the Swede Dome turnoff. The turnoff road leads to the abandoned settlement of Sixtymile on Glacier Creek. A four-wheel drive vehicle is needed to traverse the road.

Mileage Donaldson's crew took five days to run the Sixtymile to its mouth, plus an additional day to paddle downstream 50 miles (80 km) to Dawson City.

River Character The river is navigable with some difficulty. There are frequent but easily navigable rapids during low-water periods. During heavy runoff, the difficulty would increase. During the low-water periods of late summer (August), a sturdy canoe is required because the river is so shallow that the bottom would be scraped frequently. Lining, hauling and portaging are often necessary and good footgear should be worn. The river water is potable.

Suggested Reading

Atlin Centennial Committee. *Atlin 1898-1910*. A history of the area, well-researched and informative; available from the committee at Atlin and some northern bookstores.

Berton, Pierre. *Klondike*. Toronto: McClelland & Stewart, 1973. The definitive history of the gold rush. Previously published in U.S. as *Klondike Fever*.

———*Drifting Home*. New York: Knopf, 1973. An account of the Berton family's float trip down the Yukon River with flashbacks to his father's experiences in the gold rush and Dawson City.

Cantin, Eugene. *Yukon Summer*. San Francisco: Chronicle, 1973. Account of Cantin's trip down the Yukon in a kayak.

Green, Lewis. *The Gold Hustlers*. Anchorage: Alaska Northwest Publishing, 1977. The only history of the fights over placer mining in the Klondike after the stampede.

Hunt, William R. *North of 53*. New York: Macmillan, 1975. Excellent account of smaller gold rushes and off-beat facts about the Klondike stampede.

Mathews, Richard, *The Yukon*. New York: Holt, Rinehart and Winston, 1968. One of the "Rivers of America" series, well written, with most of the emphasis on the Alaskan Yukon.

Morgan, Murray. *One Man's Gold Rush*. Seattle: University of Washington Press, 1967. The famous E. A. Hegg photo collection that shows the gold rush and the Nome stampede, plus the building of the White Pass & Yukon Route.

Satterfield, Archie. *Chilkoot Pass*. Anchorage: Alaska Northwest Publishing, 1978. A history of Chilkoot Pass during the gold rush with a guide and maps to the present trail.

———*After the Gold Rush*. Philadelphia: J. B. Lippincott, 1976. A journey through the present Yukon with commentary on what has happened since the gold rush.

Wharton, David B. *The Alaska Gold Rush*. University of Indiana Press, 1972. One of the best books to put the entire sequence of gold rushes in Alaska and the Yukon into their proper perspective.

Wright, Allen A. *Prelude to Bonanza*. Sidney, B.C.; Gray's Publishing, 1976. The history of the Yukon prior to the Klondike discovery.

Wright, Richard and Rochelle. *Canoe Routes: Yukon Territory*. Seattle: The Mountaineers, 1977. Complete survey of choices for the beginner or the experienced, with maps.

Index

Alaska Highway, 1, 11, 31, 42
Anvil Mine, 75
Ashford, B.C., 6
Atlin, 9, 10, 17, 31-37
Atlin River, 36-37

Ben-My-Chree, 38-40
Bennett, James Gordon, 25
Bennett Range, 25
Big Salmon, 68
Birch Mountain, 31
Bompas, Bishop William Carpenter, 26
Bonanza Creek (Rabbit Creek), 5, 115
Britannia Creek, 93
Ballarat Creek, 93
Burian, Rudy and Yvonne, 101-103

Campbell, Robert, 3, 46, 84-89
Canyon City, 49
Carcross, 9-11, 26
Carmack, Kate, 26
Carmack, George Washington, 5, 26
Carmacks, 11, 74-77
Casca, 61
Chilkat Indians, 86-88
Chilkoot Pass, 2, 6-7, 24
Chisana Gold Rush, 93
Circle City, 2, 5
Coast Range, 25
Coffee Creek, 93
Collins Telegraph, 59
Conrad, 28
Cook Inlet, 6
Copper River, 6

Dawson City, 1, 2, 3, 7, 8, 11, 17, 109-118
Dawson, George M., 5
The Duchess, 10, 26
Dyea, 7
Dyea Inlet, 2

Edmonton, Alberta, 6
Engineer Gold Mine, 40-41
Evelyn, 65
Excelsior, 6

Fan Tail Lake, 42
Five Finger Rapids, 77-81
Florence Range, 39
Fort Reliance, 62-63
Fort Selkirk, 46, 82-93
Fortymile, 5
Fort Yukon, 88

Golden Gate, 38
Grahame Inlet, 9, 32, 37-38

Harper, Arthur, 62
Hootalinqua, 64-67
Hudson's Bay Co., 4, 84

Inside Passage, 7
Isaac Creek, 93

Jake's Corner, 42
James, Stewart (Trail), 34
Juneau Icecap, 9

Kellyville, 77
Keno, 75
Kirkman Creek, 94
Klondike, 11, 53, 65
Klondike City (Lousetown), 115
Klondike Gold Rush, 1
    Discovery, 5
Klondike Highway, 11
Klondike Gold Rush National Historical
    Park, 1

Laberge, Mike, 59
Ladue, Joseph, 5, 107
Lake Atlin, 9, 26, 31-37
Lakeview, 68
Lake Bennett, 7, 8, 17, 21, 25
Lake Laberge, 8, 11, 52-53
    Laberge Creek, 55
Lake Lindeman, 7, 24
Little Salmon, 68, 71
Llewellyn Glacier, 34
London, Jack, 48, 104
Lousetown (Klondike City), 115

Lower Laberge, 61
Lynn Canal, 2, 3, 7

McLaren, Kenneth, 9
McQuesten, Jack, 62
Maculay, Norman, 49
Malaspina Glacier, 6
Marsh Lake, 11, 28, 30, 45-46
Mayo, Al, 62
Meadows, Arizona Charlie, 112
Miles Canyon, 7, 8, 9, 47-49
Miller, Fritz, 9
Miller, George, 9
Minto, 11, 82
Minto Flats, 82
Moosehide, 107
Mounties (RCMP), 7
Mount Conrad, 27
Mount Racine, 27

Nares Lake, 25
Nares Mountain, 26, 27

Old Thirtymile River, 61
Ogilvie Island (and post), 107
Olive May, 58

Palace Grand Theater, 111
Partridge, Otto, 39
Pelly River, 3, 82
Pine Creek, 9, 31
Portland, 6

Rabbit (Bonanza) Creek, 5
Richtofen Island, 11, 55
Rink Rapids, 81
Roberts, Danny, 84, 90-91
Rotary Park, 53
Russian American Company, 4

St. Elias Range, 55, 81, 99
St. Michael, 5, 6, 8
"Sam McGee's Ashes," 81-82
San Francisco, 6, 7

Schwatka Lake, 46, 49
Scotia Bay, 10
Seattle, 6, 7
Service, Robert, 58
Shipyard (Hootalinqua) Island, 65
Sixtymile River, 107
Skagway, 8, 21
Skookum Jim, 5, 26
Squaw Rapids, 8, 47
Steele, Sam, 47
Stewart Island, 101-108
Stewart River, 5, 48
Surprise, 31

Tagish, 30, 42
Tagish Charley, 5, 26
Tagish Indians, 3
Tagish Lake, 8, 11, 25, 26, 27, 42-44
Takhini River, 11, 55
Taku, 9
Taku Arm, 28, 38-44
Tantalus Butte, 74
Tarahne, 10
Tatchun Creek, 81
Teresa Island, 31
Thistle Creek, 98
Tlingit Indians, 3
Torres Channel, 32
Tutchone Indians, 3
Tutshi, 26, 39
Tutshi Lake, 28

Vancouver, 7
Victoria, 7

Whitehorse, 61
Whitehorse, 8, 9, 31, 50, 51-55
Whitehorse Rapids, 8
White Pass, 2, 6, 7, 99
White Pass & Yukon Route, 1, 8, 9, 11, 25, 39, 40
Windy Arm, 27-28

Yukon Crossing, 82

AUTHORS GUILD BACKINPRINT.COM EDITIONS are fiction and nonfiction works that were originally brought to the reading public by established United States publishers but have fallen out of print. The economics of traditional publishing methods force tens of thousands of works out of print each year, eventually claiming many, if not most, award-winning and one-time best-selling titles. With improvements in print-on-demand technology, authors and their estates, in cooperation with the Authors Guild, are making some of these works available again to readers in quality paperback editions. Authors Guild Backinprint.com Editions may be found at nearly all online bookstores and are also available from traditional booksellers. For further information or to purchase any Backinprint.com title please visit www.backinprint.com.

Except as noted on their copyright pages, Authors Guild Backinprint.com Editions are presented in their original form. Some authors have chosen to revise or update their works with new information. The Authors Guild is not the editor or publisher of these works and is not responsible for any of the content of these editions.

THE AUTHORS GUILD is the nation's largest society of published book authors. Since 1912 it has been the leading writers' advocate for fair compensation, effective copyright protection, and free expression. Further information is available at www.authorsguild.org.

Please direct inquiries about the Authors Guild and Backinprint.com Editions to the Authors Guild offices in New York City, or e-mail staff@backinprint.com.

CPSIA information can be obtained
at www.ICGtesting.com
Printed in the USA
FSHW020508120719
59954FS